If the Trash Stinks,
TAKE IT OUT!
14 Worriless Principles for Your Success

Phoebe Chongchua

Bloomington, IN Milton Keynes, UK

authorHOUSE

AuthorHouse™
1663 Liberty Drive, Suite 200
Bloomington, IN 47403
www.authorhouse.com
Phone: 1-800-839-8640

AuthorHouse™ UK Ltd.
500 Avebury Boulevard
Central Milton Keynes, MK9 2BE
www.authorhouse.co.uk
Phone: 08001974150

First published by AuthorHouse 5/4/2006

ISBN: 1-4259-3746-2 (sc)

Library of Congress Control Number: 2006904153

Printed in the United States of America
Bloomington, Indiana

This book is printed on acid-free paper.

Cover design by Jody Lynn Photography

Lovingly Dedicated:

To my beautiful daughter, Siena:
May your life be filled with love, balance, and harmony.
Thank you for being a constant reminder of the
pure beauty that exists in this world.
I love and honor you.

To my mother, Mary Kelley:
Thank you for supporting me in this project.
I am so grateful for our friendship and time together.

To my father, Serm Chongchua:
I carry with me your compassion and caring heart.

To you, the reader:
May this book bring you peace, prosperity, and successful living.
You are important in this world, and I am honored that you have
chosen to make this book part of your life.

Contents

FIRST WORDS

One entry found for "Worriless Living"
Worriless Living: (wûr'ē, wŭr'ē)
1. **Living a successful, healthy, enriched life**
2. **Living in harmony, balance, and abundance**
3. **Infinite energy and passion to create and live the life you love**
4. **Taking out the trash before it rots!**

These are my definitions for a term I call *worriless living*. You can create a life free of worry, fear, hatred, jealousy, apathy, revenge—and instead live a balanced, harmonious, abundantly successful life filled with passion, creativity, compassion, gratitude, forgiveness, and happiness. You can *will* this into your life if you choose to—and what you *will* into your life transpires, for better or for worse.

There are people who choose to *will* into their life good things—good people, good health, good income, good living, good energy, (even good parking spots!), etc. Their lives get better and better. They are not without troubles, but when they have difficulties, they *will* into their lives all that they need to return to a highly energized and successful, healthy, enriched life. They are doing it now all around you. Maybe you're one of them. If so, then you know it takes a persevering spirit to keep our minds connected to the energy that helps us create the lives we intend to live.

Those who are on this highly conscientious path of awareness are committed to a purpose of *worriless living*—boldly living without fear, negativity, and self-destruction. You too can live this way!

However, the opposite is also true. You can *will* into your life problem after problem—if you focus on the negative and on that which you do not want in your life, suddenly you will find that it too transpires (all because you have allowed it to dwell in your consciousness and thus even beckoned it into being).

But wait, I can hear the objections now: "I never asked for trouble." Maybe not directly; perhaps you merely thought about or worried about all the bad things that you don't want to experience, thus making that a part of your daily conscious and subconscious mind. When your head is overflowing with such negative trash, you cannot make room for treasures. Think of it the way writer Ekhart Tolle explains it, "Whatever you fight, you strengthen, and what you resist, persists."

As I am on my journey, conscientiously focusing to create the life that I intend to live, I recognize an important element of the journey is sharing what I have learned and continue to learn from others. I have discovered from both my life in TV news reporting and my insatiable desire to research self-development and fulfillment that there are certain underlying principles in successful, *worriless living.* This book gives the 14 principles for *worriless living* that coincide with success. The people who practice these principles don't stumble upon success—they have created and *willed* it into their lives. This brings abundance, joy, and love into their lives. They Take Out the Trash when their lives become cluttered with that which does not serve them well. How do they do it? Successful people employ certain core characteristics. They are kind to themselves. They are optimistic, energetic self-starters. Understanding the power of a thought, they recognize that, once accepted, a thought prompts a belief and then an action. Successful people align their thoughts to support their intentions. They expect success. They quiet their minds, recognize negative self-talk, censor it, and replace it with affirming, positive messages. By assuming responsibility for their lives and lovingly caring for themselves, they empower themselves.

To Take Out the Trash, you also have to be willing to let go of negative thoughts that are self-limiting. A common thread that binds most people is a feeling of being unworthy or not good enough. Even those with highly-inflated egos fall victim to this perception. What you find, though, is that successful people have such a healthy inward image that they are not affected by criticism, rejection, and failure. Successful people do not criticize themselves or others. They let go of thoughts that do not enhance their lives.

There are three steps you can do right now to Take Out the Trash. First, take time to explore what thoughts routinely dominate your thinking. Many of us have fallen into an unsuccessful habit of thinking about what we *don't* want. Have you ever made any of the following statements? "I don't want to be fat; I hate being late; I am so tired." Replaying these messages over and over in your head will only attract more of what you don't want, more of what you hate, and more of what you are feeling.

Second, evaluate each thought as it comes into your mind and throw out those thoughts that do not support you. Turn your censor monitors on "high" so you can carefully filter out the negative, self-defeating messages from the positive, self-affirming ones. By thinking of only positive, self-affirming messages, you will find that there is no room for the negative ones. A technique for this is explained in greater detail in Principle #7, *I Create Positive Expectations.* Be aware of how often you say things such as "I hate..." Words have power; use them carefully. In Principle #1, *I Choose to be Successful,* we look at the research behind the spirit of words and the effect they have on our lives. Recognize those negative, self-defeating thoughts as trash—something that will eventually become a negative belief that will create self-inflicted limitations on your life and never bring you success.

Enhancing your life by letting go of negative thoughts is extremely difficult; a diversion is needed. You can eliminate negative thought patterns by replacing them with the kind of thoughts you want to affect your life. Our *free will* gives us the ability to express thoughts that align with either positive or negative polarities. We choose our experiences by our thoughts. For example, imagine that two people are fired from a job. One person thinks of the firing as "good"—a chance to explore other opportunities. Basically this person decides that this is a sign to move forward with other ideas that have been put off for a long time. The other person is worried and fearful, and decides that this is a "bad" life event. These people will have drastically different experiences as they work to find or create a new job. Their experiences are first created by their thoughts. How they judge a situation becomes the experience that will align with their lives.

Third, begin to collect kindly messages that support you. Being kind to yourself allows you to also be kind to others. This creates an enriched life that offers many rewards. By replacing your negative, self-defeating thoughts with messages of self-approval, you open the door to receive treasures. Good things will begin to come your way when you create a mental magnet to attract success.

Many people have a very difficult time being kind to themselves because our society teaches that loving yourself—even liking yourself—is arrogant and self-centered. Actually, if you do not love yourself, you do not have the capacity to really love others. Begin by telling yourself how much you like things about yourself.

In the remake of the 1955 film *The Last Holiday*, the main character, Georgia Byrd (played by Queen Latifah) is a shy, coupon-clipping, humble sales clerk who gives cooking demonstrations in a big chain store, but never allows herself to sample the various foods because of her constant dieting. Byrd also avoids romance, despite wanting it. She lives a lonely and unfulfilled life until she is diagnosed with a terminal illness and is given just weeks to live. Byrd's character is not unlike many of us. We miss out on life because we are worried about consequences, many of which will never come true. Byrd even has a book of what she calls "Possibilities," yet the items in the book (travel brochures, wedding pictures, and photos of delicious foods) are really things that appear "impossible" to Byrd. She never travels. She isn't successful in love because she is fearful to try, and she doesn't allow herself to eat what she enjoys. When Byrd is given the bad news, she changes into an inspiring woman who lives life beautifully. Because she only has days left, she travels, eats the foods that she had previously deprived herself of, learns to love herself, and really *lives*. Latifah perfectly portrays the reinvented Byrd as the kind of person most of us would like to be, and she delivers a powerful message through her character. At one point in the movie, when sharing her views on cremation, she comments, "Spent my whole life in a box; I don't want to be buried in one." The lessons I took from the movie were to be present in the moment, go after what you want, and be kind to yourself.

Standing in front of a mirror, Byrd begins to realize she is loveable, important, and deserving of success. In a monologue, Byrd expresses the same emotional frustration that many of us feel. "Next time, we'll do things different. We will laugh more, we'll love more. We'll see the world. ... We just won't be so afraid."

In another scene of the movie Byrd tells dinner guests, "I wasted too much of my life being quiet. I was afraid, I guess. You know how it is. You keep your head down and you hustle and hustle, then you look up one day and wonder how did I even get here?"

By the end of the movie, Byrd creates a "Book of Realities"—all the things she wanted to experience but once was to afraid to try.

Allow your mind to dwell on the good you want to bring into your life and then focus on experiencing it as though it already exists. Believe that you deserve the best. Love yourself. You're never too old or too young to start the process of successful living.

When you Take Out the Trash, you then have room for growth, development, and a place to put your treasures. However, many people won't Take Out the Trash because they are afraid of what will take its place. Some people carry around their worries, fears, stresses, and past problems as though they were trophies symbolizing their great survival in this world. The reality is that lugging around that much garbage is backbreaking work. Why do so many people do it? There are some emotional payoffs for people who don't take action to clear clutter, eliminate self-limiting behavior, change self-defeating mind-sets, and become successful. Typically the payoffs come from at least one of the following scenarios: lying to themselves (self-deceit); complaining instead of taking action; avoiding the fear of the unknown; and avoiding responsibility.

It's hard to think that anyone would consider these "payoffs" as rewards. But if you explore them a little closer, you can begin to see how self-defeating habits are perpetuated. The following scenario illustrates how self-deceit can contribute to sabotage. A woman spends months designing the perfect logo for a company she wants to launch. Her fear and worries about actually launching the company keep her focused on perpetuating the design stage so that she doesn't have to take the responsibility of the next step (which she is afraid to do) and actually launch the company. By delaying finishing the logo, she allows herself to stay in an emotional state of delusion. She tells herself, "When I finish, I'll have great success," but she is stuck in the design phase, and avoids finishing it and moving to the next level in business development. By not taking action, she is not risking failure. She is constantly telling herself, "When I get this logo perfectly designed, I'll be successful." Procrastination is immobilizing her and preventing her from experiencing true success.

Success is revealed when mental trash is dumped!

Clearing mental clutter is something you have to practice. It takes genuine effort to develop and maintain a conscientious mind that is highly filtered and filled with messages that are aligned with your intentions. Just as maintaining a good weight and healthy diet takes work, keeping a positive, *worriless life* is also a daily choice. People who learn to keep their minds focused on what they intend to have live more successfully than those who don't.

I believe we all share a social responsibility: to teach our children how to replace their negative, self-defeating thoughts with positive messages that ensure greater success. We have to encourage children to love themselves, and we have to show them how this is done. It takes a village of people who love themselves to raise a society of healthy children with high self-esteem. We all share this duty.

Every morning and every night as I kiss her I say to my 10-year-old daughter, Siena, "I am filling you up with love from the top of your head to the tip of your big toe and everywhere in between, so that you have plenty of love to give and will never be without." Siena also practices training her mind to accept only self-affirming messages that promote the things she wants to create in her life. I was thrilled to see how she had picked up these principles and applied them to her life using her own style. Before taking tests at school, she sits quietly and says to herself (or sometimes out loud), "I am getting an A on this test." Of course, she has studied and prepared. But by affirming her desire, she is creating her own reality—and more times than not, she gets that "A." Siena is setting herself up to create her own "Book of Realities" written and lived exactly as she desires.

When you teach your children and then they teach others, you know the principles of success are firmly taking root in their minds. There are times when I have had difficulty practicing what I preach. Siena gently reminds me to stop focusing on "the bad stuff" and think about things that make me feel good. She takes out an invisible chalkboard and tells me to pretend to write my worries on it. Then, with the grace and wisdom of a well-trained spiritual teacher, she uses her invisible eraser to wipe them away. She is a wonderful example and a daily reminder for me that it's worth the effort to apply the 14 principles described on the following pages; when I incorporate these principles into my life, they bring success and harmony.

Do you want to change your life? Do you want your life to be lived by circumstance, or by what you deliberately create? Do you want to be a catalyst to help develop the lives of those you love? When we understand that our lives are intricately intertwined, we realize that we must care for each other—for what we do to one another will also impact our own life (if not immediately, then in the future). Then we begin to recognize that every move we make matters to all of us. Simply by being alive, we are responsible for changes. Even though some may feel isolated, no one really is—we all have some impact on the world. I want you to believe in this most of all because our future generations depend on the things you do.

As part of my journey, I am committed to helping you actualize the life you imagine, because the greatest reward for me comes from helping people achieve their dreams. Through helping others, I build my character, develop my strengths, and learn to stop my own terrible habit of worrying. *I finally Take Out the Trash and make room for treasures in my own life.* I am still on my journey—traveling a path that has taken me through some very dark moments, left me at times yearning for familiar ground, and at other times reveling in the new and exciting spirit of entrepreneurial adventure. I fill my heart with gratitude, for when I do this there is no room for negative feelings.

May you have an open heart and mind to receive the love and goodness I intend for you, and may your journey be blessed with enlightenment.

How to Use This Book for Results!

S_ _ _ or get off the pot! Just do it! Build a bridge and get over it! If the Trash Stinks, Take it Out!

Imagine how much easier life would be if we all could just apply these simple principles. But instead of taking action, a lot of us choose to be reactionary—we wait for something to happen to us before we do anything. Too many of us get stuck in damage control mode—fixing instead of living our lives the way we want. And that can be quite a problem.

If you're a salesperson and you wait for the phone to ring instead of working to bring in customers, you'll go broke! If you have a problem with your spouse and you wait for *the other shoe to drop* before you face the issue, chances are that you'll explode instead of handling the original problem rationally. If your child isn't doing well in school and, instead of immediately addressing the situation with the teacher, you wait until the end of the year, chances are that your child's grades will suffer and you'll be more stressed and irritated. If an employee is late and you notice a pattern developing but decide not to confront it, chances are that you'll have a real headache on your hands when you finally get around to correcting the problem.

Avoidance is not the answer—action is.

Sometimes it's that simple to keep our lives on track. If something isn't working, fix it. If you're spending time with negative people, DON'T. They'll bring you down and suck the energy right out of you. If you're obsessing over negative self-talk, then TAKE OUT THE TRASH. Dump it! Because if you don't, you know what happens: trash *rots!* A head filled with rotten trash has no room for treasures.

Too many people offer too many excuses about why they can't accomplish their goals (e.g., lose weight, eat better, communicate more effectively, stop smoking, spend more time with family, work less, work more, find a hobby, start dating, get out of debt, apologize, etc.). The reality is that most people haven't learned Principle #13: *Leave the Buts Behind* or they only get bigger. Our excuses grow while our goals shrivel up and die.

Remember your dreams? What stopped you from achieving them? What obstacles did you allow to create a barricade between you and your dream life? What "buts" could you not leave behind?

Life is about choosing a path for your journey. If your feet are pointed in the right direction, then all you have to do is walk. We can create success in our lives if, just like a toddler learning to walk, we move forward one step at a time. Yes, we will stumble and fall, but if we're truly like a toddler, then we will get up and practice walking some more. And as long as we don't give up, we will eventually succeed. The principles in this book walk you through the process of creating a successful, healthy, and enriched life.

"All of your dreams will come true, if you have the courage to pursue them."

Walt Disney knew that *happiness requires action*. I love how Hollywood movie directors alert the actors, film, and stage crew that filming is about to begin with the words "Lights, camera, action!" The power is in the word "*action*; at this point the actors transform into the characters they've been rehearsing. Actors don't just sit still and let time pass them by; their job is to begin—to take *action* and make things happen.

"All the world's a stage..." a famous playwright once said.

Isn't it time you put some *action* back into your life?

On the following pages you'll see this symbol:

This represents the good that you can uncover and bring into your life when you unlock the treasure chest. "How can I do this?" you ask. The answer is: put the 14 key principles in this book *into action*.

You'll also see this symbol throughout the book:

This is a reminder for you to Take Out the Trash. When you see this symbol, stop and think about what you're holding onto in your life that isn't working, that isn't serving you. It could be a mind-set, a job, a relationship, or feelings—something that, once you let it go, you'll be better able to attract and receive success.

This symbol will remind you that no matter how much you try to cover up the trash in your life, if it sits there long enough, it will rot. The longer you delay dealing with your worry, stress, self-doubt, and negative self-talk, the sooner it will rot and cause weaknesses in other areas of your life such as your health, career, family, and relationships. When you Take Out the Trash, you make room for treasures; only then do you experience what I call *soulful success*. Try it and you'll see it's that simple to practice *worriless living* in order to have a successful, healthy, and enriched life.

Introduction

Every step we take, we change the world, be it intentional or
unintentional, through subtle ripples or tidal waves. While our actions
may be fueled from solitary choices, the repercussions of our behavior
touch those closest and farthest from us,
those we love and those we may never know.

~ Phoebe Chongchua

Over the years I've accumulated a whole lot of trash, mostly in the form of negative thoughts, self-doubt, and worry. I, like you, have many worries. Even as I write these words, I wonder—worry—about what will happen to this book. Will you actually read it and benefit from the message I intend? Many times I was buried beneath so much worry that I actually stopped writing. I thought, "How can someone who is so worried help others?" But a small voice that I believe is guided by God told me to persist. And as I did, I discovered principles that unlock treasures. So I Took Out the Trash and picked up where I left off. Each time I realized how much further ahead I could have been if I hadn't let worry accumulate like trash. I had greater success when I got busy and *kept going.*

I know many of you are faced with many fears. You worry about not having enough money, whether to make a career change, when your health will improve, how you'll make it through another day. Worry is not an easy habit to kick. But pay attention to that last sentence. Worry is a *habit.* Somewhere along your life's journey, you were actually taught to worry. You probably watched others engage in this useless habit. And like most of us, you assumed that it's what you do when you have a problem.

My parents divorced, and I battled low self-esteem as I grew up. Abandonment issues once plagued me after my mother willingly disappeared for nearly six months when I was 15. I felt absolutely helpless at times when three of my closest friends tried to commit suicide. One was barely a teenager overwhelmed with life and pressures; another, a high school friend, fell victim to drugs; and later, another friend—a single mother in her thirties—felt as though life was no longer worth living. Thankfully all three survived and today one of them is the happiest she's ever been (which illustrates Principle #8: *I Know This Too Shall Pass*).

I am grateful for all my problems. I became stronger and more

able to meet those that were still to come.

~ J.C. Penney

Life misses no one. Tragedy strikes everyone at some point; you cannot dodge it, nor can you spare yourself from it by worrying about it. But how you choose to handle tragedy defines how you'll experience life.

A very good friend in high school suffered a tragic accident and lost sight in one eye. She had been hit with a discus while I sat next to her during cheerleading practice. Just a fraction of an inch closer to her temple and the horrific accident might have killed her. She completely lost her eye, but not the will to persevere, despite the tremendous pain and numerous surgeries (not to mention the curious stares from fellow students). She told me she was glad that the accident happened to her instead of someone else because she could survive it. At that time, I didn't realize just how important that kind of mind-set was, or how vital a tool it is throughout all of life. But my friend knew it, and she chose to survive in spite of her circumstances. She demonstrated a valuable lesson: If you think you can or can't do something, in the end you'll be right.

Life consists not in holding good cards but in

playing those you hold well.

~ Josh Billings

We are all worriers—as mothers, fathers, sons, daughters, wives, husbands, neighbors, parishioners, board members, executives, volunteers, leaders, friends, etc. Each of those titles can add more worries to our lives.

Like you, I have battle scars; mine are from a painful divorce and custody problems. I have endured the dating warpath (those stories alone are enough for another book!). I've had a successful career in broadcast journalism, working on-air as a newscaster and reporter in San Diego, California for 15 years. But there were severe bumps along the way, including demotions and struggles to hold my job in a cutthroat industry.

Sometimes it takes a traumatic incident to change the way we think, the way we live our lives. For me it was the death of my beloved father in 2002 from prostate cancer. I watched a once-healthy man whittled away by the vicious killer. Suddenly I saw life from a new perspective. Guided by an entrepreneurial spirit, God's beckoning, and my life coach, Brook Montagna, I chose to venture off on my own. I left behind a secure salary and the only career I'd known, and took the risk of becoming my own boss. At the same time, I was caring for my daughter while grieving the loss of my father, and caring for my mother who had lost her husband of 22 years.

Indeed, life doesn't miss anyone.

But it's that horrible tragedy, my father's death, which also liberated me, freeing me from my own worries and building courage in a once-fearful soul. It is what I learned (and am still learning) in the valleys rather than the peaks that I hope to share with you. Through my lonely and fearful times I clung to a power within that has brought me a rich happiness despite my circumstances. And all that I have done, you can also do. All you have to do is choose. Do it now!

I can hear some of you grumbling that you've been on this earth a half-century or so and no amount of choice is going to change your life. "It's just not that easy," you say. Well, you're right. The greater the mental resistance, the fewer opportunities you'll have to lead a successful life—the life you really want. This is the way it works: The more you resist and complain, the less appealing you are to others. The less appealing you are to others, the less they want to be around you. The fewer people you are in contact with, the fewer opportunities you have. The fewer opportunities you have, the less desirable your life is and the more you feel that your life is out of your control. You begin to feel that life happens to you by chance, mistake, or accident. This is often referred to as the "Universal Law of Accident," and it basically states that you will have low self-esteem and negative feelings to the degree that you feel you are not in control of your life and destiny. How could we feel good if we felt our life is merely a series of accidents?

Accept responsibility and don't blame society, your past, or anyone else for the lack of success in your life. Take control and you'll discover that your life can be the way you choose it to be. You're never too old to choose how you would like to envision your life; it's never too soon to begin. Choose what matters to you. Choose how to respond to various situations. Choose to belong. Choose to feel good. Choose to be happy. Choose not to worry. Choose to care—about people, projects, and outcomes. Every choice you make matters, and not just to you. Once you begin, treasures are attracted to you. They come via people, circumstances, opportunities, and even challenges.

Sharp Decision

King Camp Gillette became famous because of his undying perseverance and the cutting-edge techniques he used to market his products. But his is a story of discovering determination only after he blamed society for his lack of success. Gillette's story is a reminder that when we choose to bring treasures into our lives, the results are limitless. Gillette's treasures didn't come to him until later in life—after he chose to focus on creating success in his life by inventing a product that would turn him into a millionaire. He had to first choose—set his intention—and then pursue his goal without distraction.

Gillette struggled with lack of success most of his life. His parents were innovators. His mother created recipes and his father worked in the field of inventions. His father was a patent agent. His mother published the famous *White House Cookbook* in 1887, when Gillette was 32 years old. Gillette himself had several patents, but none attracted much attention. By the time Gillette was 39, he'd written his own book, but it had a very different tone. *The Human Drift* criticized the rich and their business practices. He blamed competition for the evil in the world and proposed a utopian society that was free from socialistic pollution.

After his boss advised him to invent something people could use and throw away, Gillette (who was 40 at the time) did just that. He invented a razor holder with an adjustable head and special disposable double-edge safety blade that was considered far safer than the straight-edge blade popular at the time (which needed regular sharpening and could actually cut a man's throat).

Gillette's idea was a big success, and he eventually patented it. To increase the sales of his razor blades, Gillette gave away the razor. This marketing campaign propelled his company to even greater success; he was a millionaire by 1910.

Most of Gillette's fortune was lost, however, when the stock market crashed in 1929. Nevertheless, his story provides a simple, profound message: *Now* is the time—this moment is all that any of us have.

Choose to take action now. It will change your life. You won't do it perfectly every day. You will, however, do it better each day that you practice. Some days when I was having my own little pity-party, I struggled to try to choose to think that life could be better. I am just like many of you; fearing change and the unknown, sometimes we simply stay where we are—no matter how painful where we are is. Remember, you have the power to choose where you want to be; when you choose you create your destiny.

My will shall shape the future. Whether I fail or succeed shall be no man's doing but my own. I am the force; I can clear any obstacle before me or I can be lost in the maze. My choice; my responsibility; win or lose, only I hold the key to my destiny.

~Elaine Maxwell

Getting Started:
Reducing Worry, Fear, and Stress

The first important step is to deal with the emotions that suck happiness, hope, gratitude, and positive energy out of your body. The strongest barrier to happiness and success is the habit of running scared from your emotions. Fear will drive a wedge between what you want and what you will have in your life; that wedge rapidly turns into a ravine. In that ravine, fear and worry mix. These two emotions eventually paralyze your life, immobilize creativity, and suffocate hope. They also blind you to numerous opportunities.

Commit to change—stop letting worry, fear, anxiety, jealousy, unforgiveness, hatred, denial, and apathy run your life. Don't carry these emotions around with you. That's like carrying your trash everywhere you go. Instead, begin to be aware of how these mental states may be running—and even ruining—your life. Then think about how you can Take Out the Trash and lighten your load. These negative and self-defeating behaviors are learned. You weren't born jealous. You learned it. And you no longer have to be jealous. You can choose a different emotion. When the feeling comes, acknowledge it and let it pass out of your mind. Choose a different mind-set. You give your thoughts emotional power. Thoughts do not have the ability to control or impact your life—until you believe in those thoughts. It's when you decide to believe that you are a jealous person that you feel like one and then act like one. If you chose to let go of

1

jealous thoughts by acknowledging them and then trashing them, jealousy will disappear. You will then have greater peace in your life.

Many of us get a thought, then we put emotion/feeling into it and make it a belief, regardless of whether it is grounded in reality. We then live based on that belief. But often that initial thought was not based on truth.

Growing up, one of my clients was told she couldn't sing, couldn't carry a tune, and merely sang monotone. It took until her late thirties for her to believe that she could sing. Ironically, when she was doing some work for a film company, the camera man asked if she ever sang. "No way", she responded. "You don't want to hear me sing. I don't even do it in the shower." Turns out the cameraman worked with a lot of singers and he said that with training her voice would sound great. Sure enough, she practiced a little and began to sing around friends. The same favorable response came from them. But she had never before allowed herself to even imagine that her voice could be trained, because other people had given contrary opinions. She had internalized those opinions. They became her thoughts and quickly became the beliefs that limited her life.

You have the ability to undo a self-defeating belief and replace it with a self-affirming belief that will guide your life. You can acknowledge a self-defeating emotion and then choose a self-affirming emotion that will bring you peace. You have the power to do that.

As you'll see in Principle #6, *I Acknowledge My Emotions*, Buddhist monks observe their emotions so that they do not simply react to circumstances. They are trained in patience. They have "unlearned" the emotions that prevent successful, harmonious living. You too can do this.

When I was a newscaster I worried that if I took a vacation, I wouldn't have enough "face time" with viewers. Would they forget me or, even worse, would they like the fill-in anchor better than me? Ultimately I had no control over these scenarios I was worrying about—and the worrying really only made the situation worse because it disturbed my peace of mind. Here I was on vacation, but I was still thinking about work! Just imagine if you could live without the effects of worry, fear, anxiety, jealousy, unforgiveness, hatred, denial, and apathy. Remember that you weren't born

2

with these negative feelings. Work on eliminating them one by one, gently escorting these learned behaviors out of your life. It may not be easy at first, but the treasures you get in return will keep you focused. You will experience a positive difference in the way you view life and what you attract into your life.

Woes to Wonders—The Miracle of Danielle

Many years ago a friend I've known since pre-school had a baby. Suzy and Scott were both in their early twenties, and while she may have been ready at that time, he was nowhere near ready for parenthood. So, as ironic as it may sound, it is a good thing that life delivered what many would consider an imperfect baby.

Danielle, the couple's first child, was born with severe cerebral palsy. At the time I thought this would destroy my friend's marriage; a tragedy like this certainly could. A young couple already experiencing marital blues wouldn't stand a chance with this kind of challenge, I thought.

Danielle was hospitalized frequently for long periods. There were numerous near-death occurrences as well as surgery upon surgery just to help her live more comfortably. When things seemed to be going well, she'd take a turn for the worse. Her life expectancy was predicted to be only a few years. She would never talk, never walk, never feed or dress herself, never respond, never act like a typical child. Yet somehow this baby was filled and surrounded with love.

Several years after Danielle was born, I became pregnant with my daughter, Siena. Suzy and I sat down to catch up on old times, and she told me how Danielle had not been given proper care at birth, which resulted in her damaged condition. (Today, the couple has two other healthy, wonderful kids, plus Danielle has beaten the odds and, at the time of this writing, is already a teenager!)

The story nearly paralyzed me with fear and worry about my own unborn child. I couldn't imagine taking care of a child who would remain as a baby for life. I cautiously asked Suzy about her marriage, and only partly wanted to hear the answer. But her response shocked and surprised me. The couple was doing better than ever! Scott, her husband, had grown closer to her and their family because of Danielle's condition. I couldn't believe that Suzy and I were talking about the same person.

It wasn't until later that I saw the change for myself. When Siena was just three months old, I had to leave an unhealthy marriage (while still on maternity leave from my job at the TV station). I stayed with Suzy and Scott for a month before moving out on my own with my daughter. I was torn apart, distressed, worried, fearful, and anxious. Yet in their home I was able to smile when I saw how *woes had literally turned to wonders.* Danielle had united this family, and given them a purpose. They worked as a team, helping each other in harmony, learning lessons daily from Danielle about the mentally and physically challenged. The parents supported Danielle, the kids loved their sister, and in her own unique way Danielle showed them all that she loved them as well.

So, as the adage goes, when life serves you lemons, make lemonade.

Four Characteristics of Worry

1. Worry equals mind clutter/trash (it stinks and rots in your head, if you let it)

2. Worry is never alone—fear and anxiety are its roots

3. Worry paralyzes your life, immobilizes creativity, suffocates hope, and blinds you to opportunities and treasures

4. Worry is a breeding ground for chaos, dissatisfaction, hopelessness, and poor choices

The more you understand the destructive nature of worry, the more quickly you will act to try to lessen the amount of time you spend in this wasteful state.

The *Worriless Life Exercises* will help you reclaim your mind and develop healthy mental skills to Take Out the Trash daily and make room for treasures.

Isn't it time to take back your life and stop wasting time worrying and living under an avalanche of stress? Is there something you've been putting off doing because, deep down inside, you're afraid? Are you smothering those you love with needless worry about their lives? Whether you worry or not, life happens. But chances are that the things you worry about will never happen. Remember: When you let go of the worry, there's a world of treasures out there just waiting for you.

Our Worries

What do we worry about? Pleasing everyone, things that happened in the past (water under the bridge), health issues, money, job, love, etc. Studies indicate that most of our worries never come true. And when we spend long periods of time worrying, we are releasing chemicals into our bodies that can cause physical symptoms that range from headaches to high blood pressure. The long-term effects of worrying can increase the risk of heart conditions, as well as heartache caused by loneliness. Who wants to be around someone who is always depressed and worried?

Take some time to put your worries down on paper. Often we have so much fear, worry—basically junk floating around inside our head—that we can't determine what is really keeping us from being focused and attracting treasures. When we take time to get clear about our worries and identify if they are productive or non-productive, then we can begin to solve them without succumbing to a panic-stricken, stressed-out state.

A productive worry is one that you can *do* something about. For example, you're worried that you won't do well on a presentation you have to make at the next sales meeting. Solution: Instead of futile worrying, spend the appropriate time to research, prepare, rehearse your presentation, and meet with colleagues who can assist you.

A non-productive worry is a worry that is out of your control. Maybe you worry that your spouse will get in a car accident on the way home from work. You focus on this worry relentlessly as though worrying about it will prevent it from coming true.

Research projects have been conducted on worry. Over a two-week period, a group of worriers were asked to write down everything they were concerned about. After the time was up, 85 percent of the worries had dissolved. Interestingly, many of the worriers thought that their concern or worry about the problem became a good-luck talisman and actually somehow prevented a bad outcome. But just think about how much wasted time the worriers spent dwelling on negative fantasies—things they absolutely *didn't* want to come true.

We know that successful people think about the things they want to have in their lives, not the things they don't want. It only makes sense that if you are pre-occupied with your worries, you will not attract the things you really want. Instead, you will in fact begin to have more of exactly what you do *not* want (but are focusing on with your worry). Rather than worriedly assuming or expecting the worst, you might as well presume the best —you'll feel much happier and more confident with this attitude. Just be careful of how much you fantastically depend on winning a lottery! Remember to base your success visions on firm foundations of plans and actions.

The following exercise will help you clarify what it is you are worried about. Believe it or not, a lot of us worry about so many things that we have a constant three-ring circus going on inside our heads. You can *reduce* your level of stress and worry by defining your worries, determining if they are productive or non-productive, and then listing an action step that you can and will take immediately. Put your worries on paper to get them *out of your head.*

List Your Three Greatest Worries (productive only)

1. _____

2. _____

3. _____

List One Empowering Action You Will Take to Eliminate each Worry

1. _____

2. _____

3. _____

WHEN WILL YOU TAKE ACTION?

How About NOW?

In order to break the habit of worrying, you have to give your mind something else to focus on instead. Writing down at least one empowering action you'll take will help focus your mind on something positive that can produce effective results and, ultimately, stop the needless worrying. Here you wrote down only three, but ideally you can write down at least 20 action steps—the more, the better. As you see for yourself that there are options to your situation, your worries begin to dissipate and instead you will begin to focus on the action steps.

Another helpful tool for breaking worry is to completely understand your worries. Often when we worry, as the saying goes, we make a mountain out of a molehill. Staying grounded in the present and not allowing your mind to run off and accumulate worries in a "negative fantasyland" is vital to breaking the useless habit of worry.

Worriless Life Exercise: Challenge

Look at your list of worries. For each worry, write down at least three truths about the worry. For example, if your worry is about not having enough money, write down three truths followed by your greatest fear (which is often very unlikely to occur). You then challenge yourself to confront that greatest fear by asking yourself, "If this happened, could I survive it?" Explain how you'd survive and then list the one action step that will be your first step you'll take to reduce that worry (it can be the same action step you listed in the previous exercise).The more action steps you list, the less worry you'll feel. When I am worried, I list dozens of action steps and then work through the list to accomplish the tasks. Action dissipates worry (negative fantasy). Even if money is a huge concern, worrying about it won't bring you more money. But engaging in brainstorming sessions to produce ideas that you can then put into action is far more likely to increase your bank account.

Don't meditate on the problem; instead let your mind focus on the solution: the actions you will take to ensure positive outcomes that you intend—and then think of nothing else. Focus on what you want to get bigger, the problem or the solution.

Example

<u>Worry:</u> Not enough money.

<u>Truth #1:</u> I have the skills and ideas to make more money.

<u>Truth #2:</u> I have the contacts to assist me in making more money.

<u>Truth #3:</u> I have ample savings to last as I transition careers.

<u>Greatest fear:</u> Losing my home to foreclosure.

<u>Question:</u> Can I survive it?

<u>Answer:</u> Yes. It would be painful but, the reality is, long before I would ever be in a situation like that I would take the necessary steps to prevent it.

<u>My action step is:</u> To call my "hot leads" today, and book sales appointments with them. Also to launch my marketing campaign and meet with CEO's whom I have worked for previously to introduce my latest product.

Now it's Your Turn

Write down your top worry, then the empowering truths about your worry that will set you free from it. Write the greatest fear related to this worry. Answer the question: Can I survive it? Tell yourself how you know you will survive it, and then write down one action step you'll take right away. Remember, I am having you write just one action step, but the more you write, the less you will worry. Always take immediate action on one of the steps.

Worry: _____

Truth #1 _____

_____

_____

_____

Truth #2 _____

_____

_____

_____

Truth #3 _____

_____

_____

_____

Greatest fear: _____

_____

_____

_____

Question: Can I survive it?

Answer: YES, because _____

_____

_____

_____

My action step is: _____

_____

_____

_____

How Did We Get So Trashy?

Our society leads us to believe concepts that are 180 degrees from what our souls desire. We're told things such as:

"Don't rock the boat."

"Keep your feelings to yourself."

"Be strong."

"Don't cry."

"You should…"

"Don't be selfish."

"You must do it right, perfect."

"Never admit when you fail."

"Never do anything that will upset anyone else."

"Ignore your feelings."

"Do as I say, not as I do."

"Trust only logic, never your feelings."

"Be happy all the time."

Many people grew up with these as the "house rules." Instead of encouraging the development of healthy self-esteem and coping skills, these types of thoughtless platitudes constrict the soul, limiting human potential and making people feel guilty and thereby causing them to *conform to slogans*. These thoughts fill our heads and become the values that we operate by. As we accumulate more thoughts like those listed above, our lives become cluttered with trash and unrealistic principles that create unsuccessful and imbalanced living.

In Principle #5, *I Practice Forgiveness and Tolerance*, we learn that not forgiving and ridding ourselves of guilt condemns us to a slow emotional death that often can affect our health. Many people choose to stay in an offended state. They go through life constantly getting upset and offended by something someone has done. This allows them to be perpetual victims (who are, conveniently, not responsible). When someone offends you, you can choose to not let it get to you. But sometimes our egos tell us that we actually *deserve* to be offended. Our egos make us think that we're so important that we should feel and act offended by another's behavior, and even try to make the other person feel guilty. When we quit being offended we can successfully move on with our lives. When we stay in an offended state we are actually hurting ourselves and limiting our success. Trying to make others feel guilty indicates something inside of us is out of balance—that there's an emotion we need to face and explore.

My daughter once heard me talking with a client about egos. Siena later asked me why we were discussing egos. I asked her if she knew the meaning of the word. "Yes," Siena responded confidently. She giggled and said, "It's your bottom." I smiled and told her that that's where the ego belongs. But I was curious how she got that idea. Siena told me that she'd heard people say, "You've got a big, fat ego!"

Don't let your big, fat ego get in the way of successful living.

Much of what society teaches us to believe doesn't feel good to our soul; it just gratifies our ego. In protecting itself, the ego can create a million justifications for poor behavior. This line of thinking produces poor outcomes. The longer we keep the negative thoughts and self-defeating behaviors, the more the same are returned to us. Peace comes from examining and censoring certain emotions and thoughts. Finding peace in your life allows you to express your authentic self, or what I call "the bare you."

Go ahead: *Dare to bare it all to achieve soulful success.*

Isn't it time to Take Out the Trash and stop accumulating destructive emotions inside your head and heart? Stop carrying around the trash bag that's filled with garbage. Dump it now! It has to be getting heavy.

Are You Buried Beneath Trash?

As a news reporter, I once covered a story about a garbage man who was believed to have been buried alive at a landfill. Somehow the poor man had presumably fallen into the landfill so deeply that, despite the search efforts, he couldn't be found.

Many of us allow internal garbage to build up in our lives, and often we are the biggest culprits of filling up the trash from the inside out. We Take Out the Trash from our kitchens, bathrooms, bedrooms, and garages, and put it neatly into a garbage can outside. We then feel clean and clear. But when it comes to making an internal sweep of the clutter and trash polluting our minds and our souls, we slam the door tightly—locking the garbage inside.

The garbage inside is our worries, fears, grudges, anxieties, feelings of hatred, and unforgiveness. And like all garbage, this mixture rots, becoming even more of a mess.

If you look at the outside of a banana that's starting to spoil, you see that its beautiful yellow color is marked with black spots. But if you're really hungry and it's the only banana in the house, you might tell yourself that the spots aren't that dark. When you peel it, though, you see the true impact and depth of the spoilage. By the time the rot was visible on the outside of the banana, it had already wreaked havoc on the inside. This is what happens to you when your emotional pain remains unexpressed, unpeeled, and unacknowledged. As previously mentioned, Principle #6, *I Acknowledge My Emotions*, explores how to acknowledge your emotions but not let them run—and ruin—your life.

What is your emotional garbage doing to you? How deep are the scars of sibling rivalry; a major fight with your spouse; a confrontation with a co-worker; a hated job; a mind-set that whispers, "I am not good enough"?

When we're stuck in bad times and buried beneath emotional garbage, it's hard to ever imagine that good times are ahead.

Good moments seem to wear out and slip away quickly, while the bad times and the self-defeating emotions that come with them, such as worries and fears, are built with heavy-duty batteries—you'll wear out before they do. Not only do the old worries and fears keep going and going, but there's an endless supply of new worries in the world.

You can choose to feel better. You don't have to remain buried beneath your trash.

One of the most inspiring statements I've ever heard is so grounded in reality that it's often overlooked. The basis for Principle #8, this statement is simple: "When bad times happen, remember this too shall pass. When good times happen, remember this too shall pass."

Life is about change; whether it's good times or bad, the circumstances will eventually change. If you don't want to deal with change, get in the box; after you're dead, you don't have to deal with change or stress. However, while you're alive, choose to really live. Welcome change and challenges as an opportunity to grow and develop into the person you intend to be. Don't let the fear of change rob you of a fulfilling life. You do matter in this world; why not live fully and richly (Principle #2 *I ask, "Why Not?"*)?

To live with fear is a life half-lived ~ Spanish Adage.

Most of us would not want a job that's described like this:

"Hiring: seeking appropriate male or female to do mindless work, involving negative thinking, non-stop for hours at a time, no breaks, mindfully fatiguing, anxiety-producing with low to no positive results.

Call 1-800-It-Sucks."

This may seem outrageous, but many of us actually do sign up for that job every day (and without pay) when we give in to our worries. The *Worriless Life Exercises* take you through a process that helps you clear out your worries and Take Out your Trash so that you can make room for the valuable treasures you are currently missing.

This book is not about trying to tell you that you have NOTHING to worry about. Quite the opposite—you probably have EVERYTHING to worry about. So don't worry! I'm not going to ask you to stop doing what we're all programmed to do. Instead, I'm going to give you some alternatives to worrying. It begins with Taking Out the Trash. Just as you exercise your body to keep your heart, lungs, and muscles healthy and strong, you can also exercise your mind and diligently practice choosing the kind of life that you intend to live.

For a lot of us, our head is a scary place. There are issues, memories, painful and angry situations floating around behind closed doors. Opening up any one of these doors is like opening up a closet door where you've been stuffing in junk for decades—you never know what you'll find, or how it'll affect you now. So many of us walk by the door and pretend it doesn't exist until the over-stuffed, bulging closet door bursts wide open, spilling out everything inside.

Prevent that catastrophe by vowing to take action and examine your life before a health issue, career, or other situation forces you to do it. These *Worriless Life Exercises* and success principles, when applied and practiced, will train your mind to accept the self-affirming messages. You will begin to instantly recognize a self-defeating message and you will learn to automatically reject that thought before it takes root and becomes a belief. Those negative, self-defeating messages will no longer feel right to you. You won't worry—you'll take action!

> "Insanity: Doing the same thing over and over and
> expecting a different result."

Albert Einstein knew that to achieve different results, you had to actually *do* something differently! If your negative, self-defeating thought pattern isn't bringing you the success and harmony you want in your life, then you must think differently.

Are you stuck in the spin cycle: going round and round, and getting nowhere? Then choose and set your intention to live life differently—better than it is today.

1. I Choose to Be Successful

It should be quite obvious by now that there is a common ingredient in the recipe for success; those who are successful never reach their full capacity without seasoning their life with this key ingredient.

Simply stated, successful people consciously choose to co-create their destiny.

This is how we all start out. Nobody comes into the world saying, "I choose to be unsuccessful." The true definition of a successful person is that he or she repeatedly chooses to be successful *despite the obstacles.*

When things don't go right for successful people they don't give up. They come back with a vengeance. They have decided before they attempt to do something that they're going to succeed. When one method doesn't work, they are confident that another avenue will get them what they desire. They do not recoil from failure; they embrace it and repeatedly choose to transform their woes into wonders. We have all exercised this kind of self-discipline and ability to make persistent efforts with little things—searching until we find misplaced items in unusual places, or just trying and trying to do something until we finally accomplish it. We didn't give up; this same kind of discipline can be applied to our lives to create overall harmony. What we expect out of life is what is delivered to us. Are you telling yourself positive, supportive statements that encourage success, or are you filling your head with self-defeating, negative talk (trash that, if left uncensored, will eventually rot)?

Successful people have an affirming dialog running through their heads. Their thoughts are focused on solutions, win-win situations, achieving, being highly productive, resourceful, happy, and fulfilled. They are not focused on why something won't work. Successful people find ways to make possible things that others thought were impossible. They enjoy life. They believe they deserve their success. They choose to Take Out the Trash because they realize that garbage serves no purpose in their mission to succeed.

I chose to become a newscaster at the age of 12, and from that moment on, in my mind I was a TV news anchor. Throughout high school I was inspired by people such as Oprah Winfrey, whose childhood was filled with obstacles, yet she rose to the top, receiving many prestigious honors (including being named by *Time Magazine* as one of the 100 Most Influential People in the World and earning the Lifetime Achievement Award from the National Academy of Television Arts and Sciences). When many people told me TV news reporting was a poor career choice—too much competition, they said—I clung to the success stories and chose to believe and visualize that it was possible. I heard far more negative comments than positive ones. Somehow, though, I blocked the negative comments except to use them as a challenge to reach my goal. I concentrated on what I believed I could be, and landed my first job on the air in broadcast TV news at the age of 20 in a major market and my hometown, San Diego. I learned a powerful lesson: *Success comes to those who are willing to repeatedly choose to make it theirs, despite the obstacles.*

It is never too late to be what you might have been.

~ George Eliot

Discover WHAT it is exactly that you want to create in your life, and then *repeatedly* choose to make it yours.

An excellent technique is to wake up each morning and start your day with a success mantra—an affirming message that you program into your mind. This book is designed for you to use the mantras that coincide with the 14 principles for a no-fail action plan for your success. Don't try to do them all in one day. I suggest you read the entire book and then re-read it, practicing the 14 principles one at a time. Work on them daily for a period of two weeks. Re-read a selected principle and meditate on the mantra each morning for 10 minutes. Repeat the mantra out loud and watch how your body or mind initially responds (including trying to reject it). But don't stop, even if you are uncomfortable. Eventually, as you begin to believe wholeheartedly, your mind will accept this as your new principle to operate by. If you do this for a period of 14 to 28 days, you will see positive results and new treasures in your life. These may have already existed, but your former state of mind would not allow you to experience the success. When you have practiced and learned these principles and mantras, continue to add your own in order to support the life you want to create. Connecting to a vision (discussed below) is the critical component that sets apart the successful from the unsuccessful.

Remember also to spend a few quiet moments in the evening in a state of gratitude for the blessings of your life. Allow yourself to relax. Creativity occurs when pressure is absent. Ironically, the more you relax into this lifestyle and let your mind absorb these principles while also giving thanks and appreciating your life, the faster you will see results.

Defining Success

Defining success is the first step to creating it. It is vital to have a clear picture and vision of what you intend to create. You may not know how you'll create what you envision, but you must at least begin to see what your heart truly desires. Then, as you perform your affirmations or mantras each morning, the universe can support them through a spiritual force. Thoughts are energy. When we hold a thought in our mind we *will* the things and people we need to come into our lives to support it. This is a good exercise to do regularly. It helps you remember and connect with what success means to you. If you don't know, how will you ever achieve it? The following written exercise is a good one to repeat frequently as ideas and desires change. Even if the success vision stays the same, this *Worriless Life Exercise* helps keep us on track.

Key Questions:

What is success to you? _____

_____

_____

_____

How do you feel when you are successful? _____

_____

_____

_____

What motivates you to be successful? _____

_____

_____

_____

Which of your thoughts that you're holding on to limit your success?

1. _____

2. _____

3. _____

What three goals are most important to you? (Answer this question in 30 seconds)

1. _____

2. _____

3. _____

What three actions will you take to begin to create the life you intend?

1. _____

2. _____

3. _____

The second-to-last question tells you what you view as most important, and typically defines what success really is for you. Compare it to the way you answered the first question. Many people respond with "good health," "plenty of money," and "time with family." Successfully balancing those areas requires living conscientiously and having clearer goals—knowing specifically what you want. Being aware of your emotions, self-talk, spiritual guidance, intentions, and energy is also critically important in order to live a harmonious and successful life.

How to Stay on the Track to Success

I know that many of you have a success vision and are already quite successful in several areas of your life. That's terrific! But as life and circumstances change, we can all find ourselves getting a little off track. The road to success gets bumpy, filled with potholes, and often we go off on a detour.

Stay on track by keeping focused and constantly re-creating your vision for success. As previously noted, sometimes we won't re-examine our lives until a tragedy forces us to take a look. Then we realize that maybe some modifications need to be made to our lives to create the success we truly want.

Examining our lives and finding the areas we need to change can be about as desirable as going to the dentist for a root canal. Yet the effects can truly be life-changing. This next *Worriless Life Exercise* is a helpful indicator of the areas of our lives that need improvement. Rate the areas of your life on a scale of one to 10 with 10 being the optimum. Then write down the reason you gave that area of your life the particular rating. Next, write down the change you need to make to improve that area of your life and its respective rating. The goal is to create balance in all areas of our life. We do this by getting all the ratings closer to the 10 mark.

Balance Rating Worksheet

- Rate in each block how you feel about the categories
  (1 = least satisfied, 10= most satisfied)
- Write a brief reason for your rating
- Write at least one thing you could do to make that number change to reach a 10

Category	Rating 1- 10	Reason	Change
Family			
Nutrition			
Career/ Finances			
Exercise/ Energy Level			
Happiness			
Spirituality			
Play/Social			
Living My Passion			

The Nobel Prize was established after Alfred Nobel had died in 1896. His will left the bulk of his wealth in trust to create what is now known and regarded as the most prestigious international award for intellectual services in support of humanity.

The story behind why Nobel created such an award has to do with his great success and fame, most notably as the inventor of explosives—including dynamite. According to legend, Nobel wanted to create the award because of a bizarre mistake that happened in 1888. His brother, Ludvig, died in France, and French newspapers erroneously reported the death of Alfred Nobel instead of his brother. One paper's headline read, "Le marchand de la mort est mort"—*The merchant of death is dead.* Many speculate that Nobel did not want to be known as the master killer, and therefore created the Nobel Prize.

Think about what you want your legacy to be. What will you be known for? How does that compare to the questions you answered about success? What we choose to visualize today, we can begin to create tomorrow. We can create balanced lives when we have clarity and a deep understanding of what success means to us on a personal level.

Dream Big!

One of the best exercises I know for stimulating and reconnecting to your success vision is to simply write your success vision. Spend a little time dreaming big! Play reporter and write a success story about yourself. No holds barred—go for it! Write your own awesome success biography. Think about the meaningful things that you want to be part of your legacy. Now is the time to create and choose to be successful. Write your success vision using the information from the previous exercises.

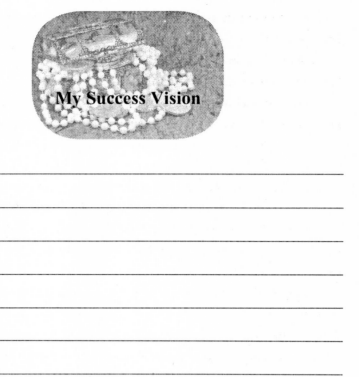

My Success Vision

_____

_____

_____

_____

_____

_____

_____

_____

_____

The importance of writing a vision is to dare to dream. By writing down a vision, you already have put yourself in a very elite percentage of the population who are truly successful. The majority of people don't write down their vision for success. In fact many can't even clearly tell you what they desire. Others keep their desires in their heads, which makes those visions nothing more than wishes—leaving them in the state of unfulfillment: wanting, but never getting.

Successful people commit their desires, their dreams, and their visions to paper. They write about their goals, talk about their goals, think about their goals, and by doing these things, they are in a perpetual state of *choosing* to create success in their lives. They do not think about the obstacles to their desires; instead they relentlessly think about how they can achieve them.

The step you just took in writing down your vision (even if it was just a brief one) is the mark of a successful person. But, just like any first effort, the more you practice it, the better it gets. By committing to writing down your visions, you will gain clarity about what it is you really desire. This gives your subconscious mind both the power and the ability to attract precisely what you want in your life. And the more you write down your visions and goals, the better you get at clearly defining and articulating them, paving the way for your subconscious mind to attract your desires.

When you state your desire and vision, your powerful subconscious mind begins to work at achieving this. However, when your conscious mind starts to doubt, fear, worry, and become anxious about your goal, your creativity is stifled, growth is cut short, and your goal appears farther away as obstacles move into view. Many people don't even bother writing down a goal or vision because, before they even can commit it to paper, they have already filled their conscious mind with trash—the reasons they can't, shouldn't, and won't be able to accomplish what they want. Their subconscious mind also becomes filled with trash and can therefore only deliver what it dwells on (in this case, *not* achieving the goal). Thus, a self-fulfilling prophecy occurs: the more that people think they cannot achieve, the greater they are at failing. Successful people fill their heads with optimism, curiosity, and eagerness to continue to reach and achieve. Quite simply, they *choose to succeed* and *believe* they can—therefore their self-fulfilling prophecy occurs with the same dynamic intensity, but in the reverse direction. Successful people attract success into their lives because of what they choose to think about and allow to remain in their heads. Consequently they live successful, healthy, enriched lives and even when circumstances present challenges, they persevere through them and come out winners.

The Power of Words

Are you having a good or bad day? What stories are you telling yourself? What message is resonating in your mind?

Think about the last time you felt really good—were you telling yourself positive, loving, thankful messages? Maybe you weren't saying them consciously, but perhaps you heard a song that warmed your heart, watched an uplifting movie, your spouse did something extra kind, or your boss recognized you for your hard work. Whatever it was, it set the stage for your mind to stay in a positive state. For hours after, your mind focused on good. Kind thoughts and gentle, loving words and phrases floated through your brain. Thus, your day was filled with goodness; difficulties seemed less irritating than usual.

We all tell ourselves stories. Some stories are optimistic and others are pessimistic. Think about a day that was good—a day when you achieved success. What words did you hear inside your head that day?

In Japan, there is a word for the spiritual state and power of words: *kotodama*. Many Japanese people believe words can change physical reality. *Kotodama* is often related to another Japanese word, *hado*—a life-force energy with healing properties (the literal translation is *wave motion* or *vibration*).

The research of Dr. Masaru Emoto was featured in the unique film *What the Bleep do We know!?* The film also featured the photographic capturing of the formation of water crystals, and the effects of both positive and negative words on those crystals.

Dr. Emoto discovered that people can project a vibrational energy through thoughts, words, intentions, sounds, and ideas. These vibrations have the power to alter the molecular structure of water.

During an interview with the scientist, he described his research findings to me, saying, "As a result we learned that when we show or say positive words, then water actually creates beautiful hexagonal crystals, whereas if we use negative words, the crystals do not form as beautiful crystals and most of them are not hexagons."

The *hado*, or life-force energy, comes from our collective social stream of consciousness. The energy resonates in each of us and is the driving force of the destiny we create. "The way we feel, the way we think is very important in creating this reality," Dr. Emoto said.

He used a special technique to capture the formation of water crystals after various water samples had been exposed to words. Dr. Emoto contends that water has the ability to retain information.

"Words we say out loud actually have energy. When you say it, it can come true," he told me.

When you recognize that our bodies are made up of mostly water, you begin to draw the connection—we too are sources of vibrations that result in positive or negative effects on our surroundings.

"When we can truly understand water, then we will come to understand two basic phenomena—which are that water is actually a medium to send vibration and also that it continues with resonance. When everything is resonating well, then there will not be any destruction, everything will harmonize," explained Dr. Emoto.

So, the next time your day isn't going so well, do a quick check to see what words are resonating in your head.

Mantra

I choose an optimistic attitude. What I focus on I will attain. I choose to be successful, transforming woes into wonders. I choose to be a catalyst, creating success in my life and the lives of those I meet—and even those I may never know.

2. I Ask, "Why Not?"

"Why not?" or "What for?" Which of these questions do you ask yourself most often? Each simple phrase conjures up entirely different attitudes and emotions.

There have probably been a few times in the not-too-distant past that you have had the opportunity to do something out of the ordinary. Maybe it was something as simple as playing ping-pong (which you haven't done since you were 10), or challenging your fitness level by hiking up a mountain, or accepting an invitation to a party, or dating someone new, or taking a different job. Whatever the opportunity, when it occurred, did you ask, "Why not?" or "What for?"

As we age, we often ask, "What for?" instead of "Why not?" And that choice creates barriers in our lives, limiting us from experiencing life richly, creating new opportunities, or just having some fun.

I have heard the story so many times—a woman wants to meet a life partner, but she spends most of her free time at home, not socializing. When she is asked to go out to events, she asks, "What for?" A mere "Why not?" may have gotten her to the event—and presented her with opportunities she wouldn't have had otherwise.

Or you may know a person like this: he's in a job he hates, but never does anything about it. He complains constantly about being underpaid and unappreciated. Maybe he wants a raise, or perhaps a new career completely, but life has dealt him disappointments, so when opportunity knocks, he can't hear it. When he's given job leads, he doesn't act on them and instead thinks, "What for?"

"What for?" "What's the use?" "What good will it do?" Ever catch yourself thinking these thoughts? Ever wish you could stop? Try "Why not?" instead. Remember, just like when we are worried, we have to find other thoughts to think about in order to replace the negative ones.

Invite opportunity into your life by allowing a new thought pattern to take up residence in your head. When you're invited to an event, or asked to do something you usually don't do (or have never done before), go ahead and ask yourself, "Why not?"

Watch children and notice how many things they do: they run simply because it's fun, roll down green grassy fields just because they're there, show emotions naturally, laugh freely,—all because it never occurs to them to ask, "What for?"

Children are naturally inquisitive, willing, and eager to experience life. Can you remember living like that? Some of us have forgotten how to go back to that place.

The next chance you get, ask, "Why not?" and then see where life takes you — maybe it'll be a new career, or just a roll down a grassy field. Either way, it'll likely provide an experience that broadens your life and keeps you searching for more interesting and exciting experiences.

Set Your Purpose

Learning to ask "Why not?" is about opening up your life to possibility. It is about understanding that, in order to live the life you want to lead, you must have intention, purpose, and desire. If you are constantly cluttering your mind with hopeless thoughts, such as "Why should I do this?", you will not connect to the kind of creativity that brings greatness. You will miss opportunity when it knocks.

Dr. Wayne Dyer discusses this topic in his book and CD program *The Power of Intention: Learning to Co-create Your World Your Way.* "As I've said many times in speeches and earlier writings, your job is not to say how; it is to say YES. Yes, I'm willing. Yes, I know that the power of intention is universal; it is denied to no one."

He also says in his CD, "By being receptive, I am in harmony with the power of intention of the universal creative force. This works in so many different ways. You'll see the right people magically appearing in your life, your body healing, and if it's something that you want—even becoming a better dancer or a card player or an athlete—the field of intention allows everything to emanate into form. And its unlimited potential is built

31

into all that has manifested even before its initial birth-pangs were being expressed."

Creating successful living requires getting out of your head and getting into your heart. There is a leap of faith that fills the gap between what we set as our purpose and how we achieve it. Many tremendously successful people did not know the way, but they were open to receiving answers.

Sometimes all you have is faith. When you stop believing and lose hope, you lose your purpose and disconnect from the essence of asking, "Why not?" Spend some time reflecting on your life and focusing on reconnecting with your purpose. Invite new ideas, information, and opportunities to come into your life, and see how much better and more successful your life becomes.

Mantra

I ask, "Why not?" I am open to receiving new ideas, information, and

opportunity—through an inquisitive mind, a soul filled with hope and

faith, I welcome the chance to learn and try things that I have never

done before. I invite creative collaboration into my life.

3.   I Know What I am Fighting For

I am not a boxing fan, but I saw the movie, *Cinderella Man*, anyway. Through the gaps between my fingers, I watched the movie's gruesome fight scenes. I knew nothing about Jim Braddock before seeing this film. But somehow Russell Crowe, Renee Zellweger, and the film's director, Ron Howard, brought me to the theater.

This uplifting film of the true story of Braddock's rise to fame and riches—then plummet to poverty and finally, just in time, back to riches again—is truly inspiring. The acting is superb. The film serves as a reminder to all of us that what we have today may or may not be ours tomorrow. *Cinderella Man* underscores the core value that I cherish—family and children first, at all costs.

The story of tragedy and despair is one many people can relate to; it will no doubt touch your heart. Movies that live longest in my memory are those that not only take me to a time and place where I can experience life through the film, but also learn or be reminded of valuable lessons. This film may reside in my memory a lifetime.

Braddock proved that moments and feelings don't define him. He was at the top of his career and then at the bottom of it, desperately struggling to keep a wife and three children warm, clothed, and alive. All the while his feelings, perhaps of hopelessness and sorrow, did not stop him from doing the right things. I don't know if this is how the legendary Braddock truly was; *but it is how I would like to believe that he was* because it gives those of us facing our own challenges faith that doing the right thing, persevering and putting family first, will be rewarded with a glorious, fulfilling life.

I've thought about this film numerous times since I first saw it. I thought about *Cinderella Man* when I was recently told that the sister of a family friend had committed suicide, but first she took the life of her five-year-old daughter. The unbearable tragedy tore open emotional wounds from my news reporting days and made me wonder how it is that people become so dejected and consumed with anguish that life—theirs or anyone else's—doesn't matter.

Many of these people live by their feelings instead of realizing that their feelings will change. Emotions are built upon thoughts, and thoughts can and will change all the time. Even the good feelings pass and give way to crummy ones on some days. But that is the beauty of life—a chance to experience it in all its fullness. Rather than judge our feelings as good or bad, simply acknowledge that they exist, but they do not have to define or limit you.

We can awaken tomorrow feeling exactly how we intend, despite our circumstances or whatever may have occurred in the past. If you know what you're fighting for and understand why you're persevering, then staying on the success track isn't so difficult. Consider the story of Oral Lee Brown, who is creating success not only for herself, but also for others.

Oral Lee Brown

In 1987 Oral Lee Brown, a real estate broker earning $45,000 a year, knew what she was fighting for when she committed herself to paying for college education for 23 first-grade students from Brookfield Elementary School in East Oakland, California. Her promise to these students in 1987 was to put $10,000 of her own money into an account each year to pay for their college expenses.

It started with one child Brown had met at a liquor store during one of her routine stops for Spanish peanuts and a soda on a weekday morning. The little girl asked for a quarter, and Brown used her last $5 to buy her whatever she wanted. The school-age girl wanted bread, bologna, and cheese—not candy—just food to get by.

This incident would forever change Brown. She was fighting for kids just like the one she met that school-day morning at the liquor store.

Brown's promise to invest in these students' future was far more significant than just her financial contributions. She knew what and who she was fighting for, so her efforts to make a better future for these children extended well beyond a financial obligation that stretched her creativity to earn and raise funds for her "babies," as she referred to them. Brown

34

took these children into her home. She had sleepovers for the entire class when they were growing up because she knew that the children were never allowed to do these types of things. They came from poor, crime-ridden neighborhoods where parental supervision was often lacking. Most certainly, no family wanted to take on the responsibility of another family's child.

Believing that children learn both inside and outside the classroom, Brown knew she had to fight for field trips. So she organized and led extracurricular activities such as visits to an Oakland A's baseball game, the Monterey Bay Aquarium, picnics—things that other children did routinely. Many organizations donated admission for these outings.

Brown stuck by the students, keeping them in school, donating her time, working multiple jobs, fundraising, and forming a foundation—all so she could touch the lives of children who might not have ever had a chance at higher education. Today, 19 of these children are college students.

Something that had been seen as impossible was possible and happening for these children—all because one woman knew what she was fighting for.

Mantra

I have a mission in life. I live successfully. I know what I am fighting for, and am committed to succeeding. I understand that at times I may feel disconnected from my purpose, but I have the power to reconnect and awaken the spirit in me that knows what I am fighting for.

4. I Take Action!

Got Worries? Trash 'em and Take Action!

Worry a little bit every day and in a lifetime you will lose a

couple of years. If something is wrong, fix it if you can.

But train yourself not to worry. Worry never fixes anything.

~Mary Hemingway

If you don't have enough of them, I'm sure just about anyone around you would gladly give you some worries. Worry is abundant in our nation; it's like a drug we refuse to give up. Many of us are worry addicts.

No matter where we go, most of us bring worry along. Stuffed somewhere in the cracks and crevices of our brain, it waits to creep out and unleash frightful thoughts about future events—most of which will never occur.

Winston Churchill said, "When I look back on all the worries, I remember the story of the old man who said on his deathbed that he had a lot of trouble in his life, most of which never happened."

Yet each of us probably has done our fair share of worrying—and some people volunteer for overtime in this area! Like drug addicts, we do it secretly, hoping no one will discover our destructive habit. And like any addiction, the unhealthy bond can be broken, especially when you realize the harm it causes.

Think of the following analogy: "Worry is like a rocking chair, it gives you something to do, but won't get you anywhere."

Then there is this one, from Arthur Somers Rache: "Worry is a thin stream of fear trickling through the mind. If encouraged, it cuts a channel into which all other thoughts are drained."

Worry stops creative juices from flowing. It eliminates possibility and hope. But the wonderful thing is, if you learn to trash your worries, you'll make room for real treasures in your life.

Action is the antidote. Don't sit and worry; take action on even the smallest worry, and you will find that you have set into motion the energy to diffuse worry.

Telling someone not to worry is like saying, "Don't look over there." Immediately, the head whips around as though you had instructed the person to look in that direction. What works better to reduce worry are these 10 directives. Practice them each individually until you can call upon every single one of them to help you through a worrisome time.

10 Directives to Reduce Worry

1. Reveal your worries
2. Differentiate between productive and non-productive worries
3. Disarm your worry
4. Commit to living without worry
5. Allow yourself to envision the impossible
6. Have a purpose
7. Help someone else
8. Challenge yourself
9. Allow freedom to fumble
10. Build on your victories

Directives and Supporting Principles to Reduce Worry and Attract Success

1. **Directive: Reveal your worries**

   Principle: Revealing and facing your fear allows you to process information more clearly. When you keep your worry/fear bottled up inside, it begins to eat away at other areas of your life, such as your health and can cause a multitude of physical ailments.

2. **Directive: Differentiate productive from non-productive worries**

   Principle: Some worries are productive and others are entirely non-productive. A productive worry might be a nagging concern that makes you worry that you left the stove on when you left the house; consequently, you turn around, go home, and see that indeed you did forget to turn off the stove. A non-productive worry is one such as this: you worry that the world may come to an end or that something bad will happen to someone you love (when there is no apparent danger). These types of worries are out of your control. Worrying endlessly about another person will limit your success and happiness.

3. **Directive: Disarm your worry**

   Principle: Brainstorm every possible solution—good and bad. Allow all thoughts to pass through your mind, but focus on the solutions. What you focus on will become bigger in your mind and in your life. One of the best ways to reduce worry is to begin to take action that will help alleviate the stress.

4. **Directive: Commit to living without worry**

   Principle: Worry can shave years off of your life, make you physically ill, stop you from reaching your dreams. Pledging to live without worry is vital in order to achieve success.

5. **Directive: Allow yourself to envision the impossible**

    Principle: What our minds envision, our physical being is drawn to; envision your destiny and, no matter how impossible it may seem, support it with your words and actions.

6   **Directive: Have a purpose**

    Principle: Giving meaning to our lives allows us to understand why we need to be successful (such as for our children). Visualizing tomorrow better than it is today gives us hope and increases our internal drive to fulfill our purpose.

7. **Directive: Help someone else**

    Principle: Worry and self-loathing take a backseat when we reach out to positively impact another's life. When you give, it comes back to you.

8. **Directive: Challenge yourself**

    Principle: Worried you can't do something? Challenge yourself to try. Whether you succeed or fail is not actually important. What matters most is the effort you make to challenge your fears. Overcoming worry is about standing up to fear.

9. **Directive: Allow freedom to fumble**

    Principle: When we stumble, fumble, and fall, we face our fears and realize that fumbles are part of life. Give yourself the freedom to make mistakes; in them you'll find fulfilling lessons to live by.

10. **Build on your victories**

    Principle: Honor victories, small or big. Reward yourself for accomplishments and jobs well done.

Apply these 10 directives to your life; they will help you attract success. Reading them once won't do it; continually practicing them will. Many of us know how critical they are to the success in our lives, yet we won't do what we need to do.

Why?

Procrastination sets in. We get in ruts and convince ourselves that it's easier to stay with our old thought patterns and old habits—until the trash really starts to rot. We don't take action because our mind is filled and immobilized by too much negative junk. Don't procrastinate. Know that you have the power to live a successful, healthy, enriched life—now choose to do it.

Beat Procrastination—Before it's Too Late!

I don't know about you, but when I don't *feel like doing something*, I can find a hundred other things I *have to do first,* even if the very thing that I don't feel like doing *really is the most important thing I have to do.*

Yes, I am a victim of procrastination. Like millions of people, I too can get caught up in putting off until tomorrow (or even the day after!) what needs to get done *today.*

If not stopped, procrastination can turn into a lifelong bad habit that results in numerous negative consequences. The root of procrastination is often worry.

Remember "all-nighters": cramming in college for an exam that you should have been preparing for weeks earlier? And now you're the room mom for your child's elementary school class and you've delayed putting together the photo collage of all the students for the yearbook, so once again you're cramming in the 11th hour to get it all done. Or maybe you have a big proposal due and you've delayed working on it because you're worried about how it will be received, and you know it's going to be a big, difficult job.

Procrastination spreads to every area of your life and leaves you with your adrenaline rushing, mind spinning, and life in overload. Some people are just so used to working in overdrive that they almost masochistically enjoy the drama of it.

My procrastination habit comes from my career as a TV reporter. In that industry, everything is subject to the cliché "hurry up and wait." Arrive at a city council meeting, then "hurry up and wait" for the council members to talk about the issue that needs to be covered. Go on a SWAT operation where a gunman is holed up, then "hurry up and wait" for the person to be dragged out at gunpoint or be talked out of the building by negotiators. In both scenarios, several hours usually passed, and then the rush was on to get the reports done in time to hit the air.

Procrastination can keep success out of reach. Finding a way to nip the lagging habit will keep you moving forward. I use a model called the "Procrastination Buster."

People respond to incentives. We take action when we stay focused on the reward we'll get at the end of our work.

Procrastination usually follows this thought pattern (although often at a subconscious level): First we think of what we have to do. We *think it:* "The lawn needs mowing." Then we *voice it,* by attaching words and even judgment: "I really ought to mow the lawn." Lastly, we *feel it* or *virtually experience it without doing it.* In other words, we imagine how it feels to mow the lawn—we attach emotion to the original thought. Then, because it's tedious work, the weather's hot outside, and the football game is on, we choose *not to do it today.* We procrastinate.

If you take that model and go through the steps: *Think it, voice it,* and then replace *feel it* with *envision it completed,* procrastination can be stopped—and the grass will get mowed. It looks great, you won't have to do it again for a while, and you feel relaxed and guilt-free while you watch the rest of the game.

Next time you're ready to put something on the back burner, go ahead and try the "Procrastination Buster": think it, voice it, envision it. *Then get it done!*

PROCRASTINATION BUSTER

Think it

Voice it

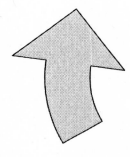

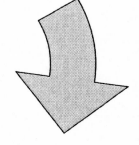

GET IT DONE!

Envision it

Hope Fuels Action

We all have the ability to take action and live our lives the way we want. But the question remains—if we all have the ability to take action, what makes one person do it and another not? The simple answer is hope. Those who take action believe that their desires will be fulfilled—they do not believe that no good will come from their efforts.

Ironically, this simple concept can be the most challenging for those who have the most opportunities for a better life—yet they do not believe it can exist—their hopes have been obliterated.

Other people think a better future is in store for them, even though they grew up with such limited resources that they had no reason to think that way. The assignments I had as a news reporter that took me to Mexico provided a pure picture of this. I reported on blanket distributions across the border a dozen times. Sometimes it wasn't blankets. It was toys, clothes, food, or even medical services from U.S. doctors operating on the cleft lips and clubbed feet of members of poor Mexican families. These people would sometimes live in nothing more than a 12' x 12' clay shack—no door, no heat, no windows, no bathroom, no kitchen—just a façade they called a "casa."

In the middle of winter, a news photographer and I crossed the border into Mexico, following a caravan of do-gooders to a remote area of the country. Our news van sloshed through mud as the wind howled, and bursts of thunder warned that more inclement weather was imminent. With seatbelts on, the van's heater blazing, we were dressed in our weather gear: boots, jackets, scarves. The truck maneuvered through the unpaved, rocky terrain to a hillside where the caravan stopped. The rain was pouring down, yet children—many who were barely able to walk and who wore hardly any clothing—rushed the vans and cars. Entire families reached out as the volunteers from various organizations began rapidly handing out blankets, diapers, toiletries, canned goods—the essentials that most of us buy daily, yet never consider what it would be like to live without them.

43

The photographer rolled video tape capturing the smiles, the tears, the hope on the faces of the young and old. It was a good day for them.

When supplies ran out, the volunteers promised to return one day with more. I had met a family who graciously invited the photographer and me back to their house. Looking for an engaging story that would show TV viewers the true picture of the need for more help, we went to their home—a tiny adobe shanty. A volunteer interpreter joined us.

It wasn't the interviews with the parents (who had been struggling in poverty for many years) that brought me to tears. It was seeing the family lovingly interact. The children quickly laid out their new warm blankets on their makeshift beds—cardboard boxes and bags. They were happy knowing that they'd be warmer than they were the previous night. They were a family with hope, a belief that God would provide. To an outsider, there was nothing in their house that gave even a glimmer of hopefulness; yet this family had built their future on the distinct certainty that tomorrow would be a better day. They trusted. They had confidence and they never gave up their hope.

Mantra

I take action, no matter how small or big. I recognize that everything I do matters to my life, to those I know, and to those I may never know. I am responsible for my choices and behavior. I make decisions and take action in a timely fashion.

5.   I Practice Forgiveness and Tolerance

No matter how you've been wronged, justice can only really be satisfied *from within*. It's a tough concept to grasp. Most of us want someone to not only acknowledge how we've been wronged, but to actually bring us vindication, reparation, and justice—to serve it up as though we were being handed back time, *actual moments* that preceded the injustice. That's not possible. Yet we believe it will make us satisfied.

Justice, however, really only comes from within. I first saw this principle in action when I was covering the murder trial of a high school cheerleader—a tragic story that seemed to epitomize our broken world. The teenager had been brutally murdered in her own mobile home, stabbed to death while her mother was away one afternoon.

How can enough justice ever be served for such a horrible crime? The mother, single, alone, and devastated, seemed at times to have a peacefulness about her. I couldn't imagine how anyone could experience peace during such a severe and unjust tragedy. But this mother was truly amazing. Her justice didn't come from a courtroom, a judge, a jury, or even the possible execution of the murderer. She seemed at peace with her life and sought to turn a devastatingly painful situation into good by creating scholarships in the name of her daughter.

When you seek the outside world to right the wrong you feel on the inside, the outcome will never suffice. You'll live life with a void, always waiting to be patched up. Seeking justice is a bitter struggle with destiny and irony. Often the justice/closure comes after someone either no longer seeks it or is no longer alive.

My father was from Bangkok, Thailand, and sadly it wasn't until after he died that I understood how he dealt with injustice and its offshoot emotions: anger and unforgiveness. My father, a Buddhist, was often quiet when people wronged him. He would typically not react, as so many of us do. When he was hurt or angry, he would sometimes exercise silence and patience, letting time resolve his injustice. Although he did have occasional angry outbursts, he'd learned to mostly "turn the other cheek."

Buddhists view anger and hatred as being based on projections from the person who has these emotions. They are not based on clarity or wisdom, nor do they serve to enlighten your life. Even worse, karma operates from the premise that the misery we cause others will eventually be aimed at us—it is our reality, either positive or negative, depending on what we choose and the way we live our lives. Remembering this helped me become more tolerant and seek to find justice within, instead of fighting for justice to be served—which can often be a losing battle.

Holding on to anger is like grasping a hot coal with the intent of

throwing it at someone else; you are the one who gets burned.

~Buddha

The following legend about a bag of nails depicts the destruction that anger does to us internally and illustrates the idea that the way we think and behave determines the success we will achieve.

A Bag of Nails

A young boy had a very bad temper. His father, attempting to teach his son patience and tolerance, gave the boy a bag of nails. He told his son, "Every time you lose your temper, hammer a nail in the fence."

Without question, the boy did so until 37 nails were in the fence at the end of a single day. As the days went by the boy began to hammer fewer nails into the fence. It became easier for the boy to control his emotions and angry temper than it was to drive nails into a fence every day.

A day finally arrived when the boy no longer needed to hammer any nails into the fence; he had controlled his temper all day. He proudly told his father. The father then had the boy pull out one nail for every day that his son had controlled his temper by exercising patience and tolerance.

Finally, after many weeks, the boy was able to show his father a fence with no nails—every single one had been pulled out.

The father then explained to his son, "Look at the fence—it will never be the same. Angry, vicious comments result in scars just like puncturing someone with a knife. As nails go into a fence, sometimes with one hard hammering, so too, angry words rapidly come out of our mouths. But when you remove nails it can be difficult—tearing away the wood and leaving holes. Your angry words are like nails: no matter how many times you apologize after they are said, the hurtful wounds remain."

What anger and unforgiveness do you need to trash? Dump them now!

Suggestions to help get rid of guilt, and forgive yourself—or another

- Write a letter describing your feelings (you don't have to send it)

- Say you are sorry or accept another's apology

- Recognize that all humans are flawed

- Think of how you would like to be forgiven

- Imagine yourself being forgiven

- Forgive others (even those who are no longer living)

- Realize that forgiveness does not mean you accept or support the action, but choose to no longer let it occupy space in your brain

- Understand that refusing to forgive yourself or another is destructive to you

- Forgiveness releases you from the hold that another person's behaviors or actions have over you

- Stop wanting to punish someone by withholding forgiveness

- Allow time to experience your emotions, then decide to move forward and leave those feelings in the past

- Forgive in order to de-clutter your life, remove excess baggage, Take Out the Trash, and lighten your load

Write the bad things that are done to you in sand, but write the good things that happen to you on a piece of marble.

~Arabic Proverb.

Differences—if Respected—Bring Togetherness

I was doing research for an article recently on Match.com when it occurred to me that peoples' differences, if they were respected, could actually bring togetherness.

What I saw on the site were people's views of how they see the world, themselves, and their ideal date. Most of the candidates told of their likes and dislikes in hopes of finding someone just like them—similarities, they seemed to believe, would bond them and keep them together.

This concept appears truly logical, but I would like to take a moment to explore the differences—that place where two people don't see eye-to-eye, the space where being different raises our intolerance, makes us irate, disrespectful, and diminishes our compassion for one another. The differences that lead us to believe we should separate, divorce, no longer be friends, start world wars—hate each other.

Lori Mitchell wrote a delightful children's book that addresses this issue; the title of her work is appropriate: *Different Just Like Me*. There are times when we display our differences, and they're met with raised eyebrows, glares, even a disapproving tone of voice that coveys the message: *conform and see it my way.*

Renowned speaker and author Stephen R. Covey once remarked about the need for disagreement, saying "If two people have the same opinion, one is unnecessary." In his book, *The 7 Habits of Highly Effective People*, he encourages readers to celebrate differences and welcome the learning opportunities they provide. When you disagree with someone, Covey suggests using this phrase: "Good, you see it differently. Help me to understand."

I've long thought that seeking *first to understand and then be understood* would smoothly pave the communication highway that was once badly potholed and marred by hurtful words. Understanding, compassion, and tolerance are tools of peace; they help end communication breakdowns that rapidly trigger hostile emotions.

Our family's and culture's conditioning heavily influences the way we see things. Together we can look at the same object, but see multiple visions. Isn't that a beautiful thing? Remember the famous French saying, "Vive la différence!"

When I feel there is only one way, someone will always show me another path. Some days I'm happy to journey along, stumbling down the winding route, uncertain of where it goes, but still willing and open to receive. And then there are times when I'm stubborn, believing I've been there, already know, or not understanding how anyone else could travel such a seemingly erroneous path. That's when my mind has closed off opportunity, pulled away the welcome mat, and imprisoned me in my own familiar routine. That's when I know I've failed to connect with a part of me that wants to learn; rather I've been taken hostage by psychological emotions that stem from being fearful, worried, judgmental, and anxious.

Fortunately, there aren't many days like that. When they come, I merely acknowledge and then let the feelings go to make room for those positive emotions and understanding that serve me well.

Mantra

I open my heart to forgiveness and know that justice comes only from within. I hold only the precious memories that serve me well. I practice patience, tolerance, and understanding—I am completely successful and richly rewarded when my heart is open to receive.

6. I Acknowledge My Emotions

When we don't allow ourselves to acknowledge our emotions, we often run from them, delaying opportunities to become more truly aware of who we are, what we need from life, and what makes us happy. Not acknowledging our emotions also compromises our ability to make decisions that are fully conscious and mindful.

I saw a tremendous amount of tragedy as a reporter. Every day it was my job to cover the bad things, the horrific incidents that made 90 minutes of evening news. I was so young and untouched by tragedy, having never experienced it or had to deal with real personal loss, that I didn't know how to process the devastating experiences that plagued so many people's lives. I often couldn't even bear to see or admit to myself the emotions I felt while covering grotesque stories.

I thought that after I stopped reporting on tragedy the incidents I covered would evaporate from my mind—memories of children abused, killed, drive-by shootings, fire scenes that wiped out hopes and dreams as they ravaged entire neighborhoods. Instead, the memories of those stories filled my head more consistently than when I was immersed in them.

I wondered why.

You can't run from your emotions; life will force you to recognize them and acknowledge them—now or later.

There was a period when I didn't ever take time to feel the emotions, because it would have hurt far too much. Reporters, photographers, and police officers joke about the tragedy they see at crime scenes. Using humor to thwart emotion allows them to do their jobs. After all, who could report on a brutal death of a child without falling apart? Our only defense was to go into a survival mode and not allow ourselves to recognize our emotions at that moment.

Suppressing your emotions is devastating to your success. However, overreacting is equally damaging. Remember the Bag of Nails story? People have learned to do damage control because of our emotions. In other words, once we can no longer suppress our emotions we lose control of them, *fly off the handle*, and then we have to mitigate the damage.

Buddhist monks are often viewed as having the ultimate control of their emotions. They don't run from, or hide, their emotions. Instead, they are trained over decades to recognize and see their emotions, yet not react to them—giving Buddhists the ability to weather tragedy perhaps better than most of us Westerners. Buddhist monks are trained to recognize the emotion or spark that ignites the flame or reaction. Their response can then be thoughtfully premeditated, rather than a mere reaction.

For most people, emotions have become automatic responses— especially in situations where there is little time for deliberation. Ironically, when people run from acknowledging their emotions, their emotions are actually running their lives.

Acknowledge your emotions, but don't be a slave to them. The following Buddhist principles can be used for guidance, regardless of your religious preference:

- *Loving kindness overcomes anger*
- *Compassion can take away suffering and overcome cruelty*
- *Sympathetic joy overcomes hatred*
- *Non-judgment (non-attachment) overcomes prejudice*

Don't Let Guilt Poison Your Soul

Guilt is an emotion that can literally poison your life. Some of us become so consumed by guilt that we can hardly function. We become embarrassed or remorseful by how we behaved inappropriately. We continuously think about how we made a mistake. What is important to understand is that we are not our behavior. We behave in certain ways to get our needs met. Just as two people may behave differently when they are faced with the same situation such as getting a flat tire. One person might immediately become very angry over the delay, while the other person might simply call a tow-truck, then read something enjoyable, while waiting, and make the best of a few quiet moments. If you do not like a particular behavior in yourself, you can choose to change it. You needn't feel guilty about it. Instead focus on loving yourself to increase your self-esteem—your unfavorable behavior doesn't make you a bad person—with your loving guidance it can be changed.

Worriless Life Exercise

Take a moment to thoughtfully answer these questions:
1. What guilt are you hanging on to that you would like to let go of now?

2. What are you getting by holding on to the guilt?

3. Are you willing to admit and accept the action that has caused you to feel guilty and move on?

4. If not now, when?

5. What will you do today to forgive yourself or someone else?

6. How will you feel when you forgive yourself or another?

7. Are you ready to let peace in to take the place of guilt or bitterness?

Mantra

I acknowledge my feelings as part of life's experiences. I choose my reactions. I am mindful of my feelings and know that they can easily be ignited. But, through careful consideration, I select the behavior and thoughts that guarantee me successful living.

7.   I Create Positive Expectations

How we see the world is how we experience it. Our expectations determine how we live our lives. If you believe that people will take advantage of you, then you will attract those types of people. If you believe that relationships don't work, then your relationships will always be challenged and will eventually fail. The reality you create in your head is what you will attract. You will create a life that validates your beliefs.

Do you complain and turn even a simple task into a painful burden? Do you think the world is filled with bad people? Do you believe that when you attempt to do something new, you will fail? Do you tell yourself stories, such as: I'm too old; I don't have the skills to do that; I am too fat or too thin; I am uneducated; nobody would want to be around me; I don't have enough money; I don't live in the right place? What other stories have you have decided to claim as beliefs? These notions are what create your experiences in life.

An elderly client, when asked to do even a simple task, frequently says, "I hope I know how to do it." The task can be as easy as turning off the coffeemaker. But before she even gives herself a chance to succeed, she has already begun to doubt herself and accept the possibility of failure.

If you want to experience life richly, then live richly. I don't mean spending a lot of money. I mean believing right now that you deserve to be—and already are— living richly. You've heard the saying "If you want to be successful, dress the part." Believe wholeheartedly that you are successful. Your subconscious mind takes its cues from what you create in your head. If you create a poor vision for your future—so it will be. If you create a dynamic vision—so it will be.

Successful people believe that everything they set their minds to will work out one way or another. They are relentless in expecting success.

You may know someone like this, or maybe you're this type of person. Everyone else calls it "luck"—they say the person was born with a silver spoon in her mouth or under a lucky star. They think that life just works out for her; even when things go wrong, the circumstances somehow create better opportunities.

You see, before I ever knew that I would write a book about getting the trash out of our heads in order to succeed in life, I was practicing the very principles described on these pages. No one had taught them to me; no one had told me to follow these principles. As a child, I somehow knew that, to survive, I had to believe. I simply believed in these principles strongly enough to create my own reality. The three principles I believed in while growing up were: 1) Imagine it and you can achieve it; 2) I never fall; and 3) I always get front row parking—a great belief to have (especially when you attend San Diego State University!).

I'd like to share the following story as a way of illustrating this point. I went ice skating with my daughter. We were skating fast when suddenly I fell—hard—landing directly on my right side. In addition to the burning pain, I instantly had a flashback—I remembered a belief that I had held while I was growing up: I never fall. Where had that belief gone? That belief, along with a few others, was critical to my health and finances.

Growing up, I was a gymnast, a cheerleader—the flier, always at the top of the pyramids and always being tossed in the air—and a hula dancer; falling even just once could have seriously injured me while brutally bruising my ego. My "I never fall" belief served me well. As an adult, though, I lost the belief and, in fact, became afraid of falling. As a child I thought, "I never fall"; as an adult I thought, "I hope I don't fall." My grown-up belief reflected less confidence. See the difference? I attracted what I thought and created in my mind. That day on the ice I focused on falling and was afraid that I would, so I did.

Throughout your journey, you will not always believe. I lost some of my beliefs during times that were extremely emotionally taxing, such as when my father died. You may be wondering if holding a belief firmly planted in your mind really works to create your reality. I assure you it does. But I also assure you it will not work for you unless you participate, practice, and persevere at it without exception. Falling on the ice made me realize that I'd gotten off track. I no longer believed that I never fall.

Changing the way you think about something will change the way it appears in your life.

This works for everyone. If you're trying to lose weight and you think about how fat you are, you won't lose weight and you'll find it hard to stick to diets and exercise routines. Instead, think and create what you wish to attract. Think about the new you: thin, healthy, and physically fit. Think of the fat melting away. This type of thinking will open up possibilities. You'll find that exercise is more enjoyable, and you'll discover foods you like that are also good for you. Don't belittle the person you see in the mirror; in time that person will emerge at the perfect weight. You'll believe it can be done and therefore you will do it. You will experience what you create in your mind.

Do you have money problems? Do you sometimes (or frequently) think about how little money you have? Then you will experience more money problems. Instead, think about what you wish to create, and then practice Principle #4: *I Take Action*. The more you dwell on your financial follies, the deeper you'll fall into money troubles. Choose to see your economic life better than it is today, and your mind will open up to endless possibilities for earning more money. Then you'll need to apply Principle #9: *I Answer the Door When Opportunity Knocks.*

Mantra

I create positive expectations. What I desire I will acquire. What I believe, I will live; therefore, I fill my mind with thoughts that support my intentions of successful living. I surround myself with optimistic people.

8.   I Know This Too Shall Pass

The essence of this principal is simple: do not operate your entire life based on what you feel today, because how you feel right now may not be how you will feel tomorrow. You might feel really good on a particular day, but you may not feel that way 24 hours later. The reverse is also true. And yes, those feelings too shall pass.

The circumstances that are creating hardships for you today will change. You have the power to change your thoughts, which can change your actions, and then your circumstances. Believe that this too shall pass; all you need to do to validate this is review your own life. Nothing has ever stayed exactly the same, has it? An essential quality of life is that it changes all the time.

Sadly, some people get stuck in the bad feelings, and make monumental decisions based on them. As previously mentioned, three people who were close to me attempted suicide. It saddens me to think that people get so depressed that they no longer value life.

I was sitting in church one Sunday morning after struggling to write a story about the importance of Principle #8: *I Know This Too Shall Pass*. Much of my inspiration, education, and hope come from Pastor Bob Johnson from Canyon Hills Community Church. I've laughed, cried, and been challenged to grow spiritually and emotionally while listening to him. So, it's not unusual for me to attend a service and leave inspired and contemplating the meaning of life. But on this day, Pastor Bob delivered a story about God that *really* spoke to me.

He told the story of English poet William Cowper, who lived about 200 years ago. As was typical, after Pastor Bob's brief mention of him in the sermon, my curiosity was piqued and I was driven to research and explore this great poet's life. I learned that Cowper suffered greatly—mentally struggling with madness, feelings of being irrevocably damned and yet at other times hopeful and feeling that God was hearing him.

Many stories exist about Cowper's depression and doubt. He tried to commit suicide repeatedly. The details of his suicide attempts differ slightly, but the outcome was the same for all—they failed or were thwarted. Stories are told of Cowper attempting to drown himself in the Thames River. According to one story, he called for a cab, but the fog was so thick that it prevented the driver from finding the river. Another version of the story indicates that the driver recognized Cowper's despair and intention and, instead of taking him to the river, deliberately got lost and returned the poet to his front porch. Another suicide attempt involved his trying to take a poison, but one author writes that his fingers were "closely contracted" and "entirely useless." And another divine intervention is also recorded: When Cowper tried to hang himself, he fell to the floor and was found by a servant.

Cowper's feelings seemed to change frequently. He came to God during his stay in an asylum and found hope. It was in the last two decades of his life that Cowper's most significant literary work was written. Throughout his life, despite his melancholy and despair, he was given reasons to live. He became great friends with evangelical clergyman John Newton (who composed "Amazing Grace") and collaborated with him to write many famous hymns. Cowper also wrote *The Task*, which is characterized as "one of the happiest accidents in English literature."

This story touched me. Here's a man who had so much to offer and yet repeatedly tried to take his own life. He may not have known at the time that his writing would touch many. His hymns, such as "God Moves in a Mysterious Way," are sung in churches everywhere—making people feel better and closer to God. Wherever we are in our lives, whether there is suffering or happiness, *this too shall pass.*

If you are contemplating taking your life, seek professional help now. You don't have to suffer—and *you are not alone.* Tomorrow can be brighter for you and, most important, you need to know—whether you feel it today or not—*you do matter.* You have a place and a purpose in this world.

Mantra

I know that I will survive. In fearful or sad moments I remember that this too shall pass. I remember my moments of joy and can reconnect to them. I focus on solutions that bring greater success into my life.

9. I Answer the Door
   When Opportunity Knocks

Sometimes after a great tragedy, loss, or failure we feel that we no longer have opportunities. That's not the case. What happens is that we are temporarily deafened to hearing the knocks of opportunity.

My father died at the age of 72—too young to leave this world.

For all its certainty, mortality is highly unpredictable. People never know how they'll handle death until it blatantly, unremorsefully shoves its way into their lives.

You kick and scream, get mad at God, turn on family members, shirk your responsibilities, retreat to quiet corners, drink a potent dose of liquid medicine, flush out memories in a desperate attempt to stifle pain—but the emotion of agony will have its say.

For many months after my father's death, sadness filled my heart. God knocked at my door in an effort to help, but I never heard because I was deafened to the knocks.

I isolated myself and fell deeply into depression, wondering why God was on hiatus when I needed him most. I thought about my father and cried alone nearly every night.

God knocked a little louder.

Two years later comfort came in the form of routine—softball games, Girl Scout meetings, bills to pay, articles to write, laundry.

Finally I heard God's knock, and I gratefully received the peace and courage that had been missing from my life for so long. I was then ready to meet my challenges and find my treasures.

12 Tips to Help You be Ready When Opportunity Knocks

1. Get emotional support in difficult times from counselors/friends

2. Be patient and allow yourself time to grieve, but begin reading inspiring material

3. Quiet your thoughts so you can hear opportunity knocking

4. Don't be overly critical of yourself

5. Always be ready to take action; opportunities often aren't planned

6. Network with others and let them know your intentions

7. Expand your horizons: take educational and personal development classes

8. Have a positive attitude; be a team player

9. Keep your commitments

10. Understand that small things can turn into large opportunities

11. Realize that no matter how successful you may be, you still need others

12. Help others: volunteer, serve, get involved

When You Do What You Love, You Hear Opportunity Knocking

One night I was eating at a local Asian restaurant. It was a fairly busy night for the restaurant and I wanted an unusual tofu order—something the restaurant could easily make, but it was not on the menu. There appeared to be some confusion about my order after the waiter told the chefs what I wanted. The restaurant's manager, Mike, straightened it out. I was sitting at the bar in front of the open-style kitchen and watched how the confusion was resolved. My dinner was delicious, some of the best tofu I've ever had. Mike began talking with me about the tofu. He was obviously proud of the restaurant's food. He told me that the tofu was a special kind that many places didn't use. Then he did something that made me a customer for life—he brought out a package of tofu to show me the brand, and began telling me where to buy it and how to cook it. He asked, "I'd like you to try another tofu dish we make; it's excellent. If you have the time, could I have it fixed for you right now?"

Unfortunately, I wasn't able to stay; I was already late, so I had to pass. But the time Mike spent talking with me will not pass from my memory. The care he took in explaining the way the food was prepared and how I could make the dish I like so much at home showed that, even on a busy night, Mike knew that happy, satisfied customers are the best marketers for the restaurant. As I was leaving, Mike came out from the kitchen and gave me a package of tofu. "A gift, so that you can try it at home. Remember how I told you to slice it."

I also go to a local grocery store where a certain employee transforms the routine shopping experience. He's known as "Gus" and I cannot think of a single time in the many years I've shopped at this store that this employee ever had a bad attitude. He must have been born smiling.

Gus isn't the manager of the store, nor is he the CEO. In fact, Gus rides his bicycle to work through a crowded upper-scale parking lot filled with vehicles such as Mercedes Benz, BMW SUVs, and Escalades. From what I can see, he puts in a lot of hours working diligently to make shoppers come back to this particular grocery store. If you've shopped there with your child, Gus has perhaps come to your rescue when your child became cranky. He pulls stickers from his pocket; children's faces brighten as he hands these to the kids. Once Gus knows that you have a child, if you're shopping alone, he'll give you a sticker or two to take home. If Gus sees you from across the store, his face will light up with a big smile, he'll give you a friendly wave, he'll greet you by name, warmly and genuinely—making you feel as though you're an important part of his day.

This doesn't happen in any other store. You can buy paper towels, fruit, and veggies anywhere. But you won't find this style of service everywhere. Gus has a style that brings me and other customers back. It's a small-town feeling that's welcome in a big city where frequently no one knows your name.

No matter what your business is, great customer service should always be on the menu and it should never go out of style.

The preceding two stories are more than just tales of great customer service. They are stories of people who recognized that opportunity was knocking—and they chose to open the door every time. They greet each day with gratitude and they welcome opportunity with open arms. Each customer is the sound of opportunity knocking—successful people always answer the door.

Mantra

I have many opportunities and my options are plentiful.

I invite good things and good people into my life,

and then gladly open the door to receive them.

10.   I Take My Eyes Off the Rearview Mirror

Think of your car's rearview mirror—notice how small it is compared to your front windshield? The latter is much larger. But many of us have our eyes glued to the rearview mirror when our focus actually needs to be straight ahead of us. Instead, we choose to hold on to past events and others' opinions of us.

Maybe you think you're clumsy, unable to learn quickly, or can't carry a tune. When you hold on to those beliefs, they dictate the way you experience life. For instance, maybe you were told that "It's your fault" when you were growing up. If you allow yourself to believe that thought, it will condemn you to a life of feeling guilty regardless of your circumstances; you'll be the type of person who constantly says, "I'm sorry." Maybe you learned growing up that "there's never enough." People who subscribe to that ingrained notion find themselves barely getting by and constantly in debt.

If you believe something, it seems to be true in your world, regardless of whether or not it really is (see Principle #7, *I Create Positive Experiences)*. Many of us form a majority of our beliefs based on what we were told as children. The opinions others had of us become our core beliefs about ourselves and, as a result, most of us are very hard on ourselves. What do you see when you stand in front of the mirror? Do you like that person? Most people will criticize and always find fault with themselves.

Working in television is a big challenge for someone who struggles with self-worth, because it is a career that includes an extremely high level of criticism (second only to Hollywood).

In the early years of my TV career, every time I'd see myself on camera or hear my voice, my first thoughts immediately went to self-criticism. There was either something I didn't like about my appearance, or I thought there was a better way I could have reported the story. It took me many years to be able to watch myself and not pick at what I thought were my flaws.

Chances are you're doing this too, all the time. Why can't we gain better control of our thoughts and lead the lives we want? A lot of us are busy stuffing our heads with negative self-talk just as we stuff garbage into our kitchen trashcan. It's not empty egg cartons and dinner scraps; instead, it's the damaging words that we have repeatedly heard and/or said to ourselves (trash!) that accumulate in our heads. And just like the kitchen trash, if you don't take it out and dump it—it will rot!

Remember, if you don't Take Out the Trash and stop cluttering your mind with negativity and worry, then there will be no room for treasures.

It's not just about negative words. Most of us have stuff floating around in our mind that weighs us down, keeps us from exercising, completing a project, visiting a relative, playing with the kids, attempting a goal, going on a diet, relaxing, you name it. A cluttered mind lets junk stay rent-free in your brain.

There is, however, a price to pay when we allow all the negative garbage to occupy space in our heads. Negative garbage is thinking that says, "I'll never lose those extra 15 pounds" or the "I can't finish that project, I'm not good enough to do it." It's all that internal talk that resonates inside us. And sometimes it doesn't just talk to us—it actually screams at us.

I'll bet right now you have at least one belief in your head that isn't serving you.

Why aren't you letting go of it? Why not replace it with one that does serve you?

Remember the story of how I became a newscaster? If my mind had been cluttered with negative chatter, I would never have succeeded. You can't have Dreams, Purpose, and a Dedicated Plan—what I call "DP-DP"—when you haven't Taken Out the Trash. Your mind is just too full, too cluttered.

One man made Taking Out the Trash a personal mission, and it created great wealth for him. He understood there are two important things about trash—people want it taken away, and they don't want to see it.

At 26, Tom Fatjo, Jr. knew how to literally Take Out the Trash. He needed his weekly garbage removed, and the people doing it did such a poor job that Fatjo took action. He bought a truck and hauled trash out himself in the wee hours of the morning; then he would go to his job at an accounting firm. Before long, others wanted him to take away their trash as well. He became a pioneer of trash-hauling services.

First at a local level and then nationally, Fatjo earned his riches by Taking Out the Trash and standardizing the industry. Browning-Ferris Industries is now the IBM of trash, thanks to Fatjo.

But if Fatjo had let negative talk bring him down, he never would have built an incredibly successful solid-waste-disposal firm.

The important thing to know about Taking Out the Trash is that it's often a messy job. So, too, is getting rid of the negative chatter that exists in our heads. Our minds resist; we might even experience some temporary difficulties and hardships as we begin to establish new principles and beliefs. It's similar to starting a prescription. Medicine can sometimes worsen your condition before it actually makes it better. But as you keep taking it, you begin to see results.

The more you study these principles, the more they'll improve your life. These principles work whether or not you choose to put them into action in your life. Like the sun rising and setting—regardless of whether you choose to take the time to watch—it does it like clockwork.

Author Louise Hay gives a fabulous analogy of how you clean your mental house in her book *You Can Heal Your Life*. She equates cleaning out negative thought patterns from our minds to cleaning up after a big Thanksgiving dinner. When you start to clean the dirty turkey pan, you need to put it in water and soap and let it soak. Then, when you start to scrub it, you have a big mess that looks worse than when you started. But if you keep scrubbing, eventually the pan will be clean again.

Hay explains this is the same as trying to change an old, over-baked thought pattern that no longer serves you. When you soak your mind with new, powerfully positive thoughts and ideas, you're likely to initially experience residual garbage that will rise to the surface as it is being exposed. Keep at it, though. Keep cleaning. Keep Taking Out the Trash, and eventually you will break your old thought patterns.

Take Out the Trash, make room for treasures.

Mantra

I recognize that my past is behind me and that now, in the present,

I create my destiny. I clear away old, negative mental clutter and

accept new, positive messages in its place.

11.   I Turn Rejection into Direction

Care for us and accept us—we are all human beings.

We are normal. We have hands. We have feet.

We can walk, we can talk, we have needs just like everyone else

—don't be afraid of us—we are all the same!

~Xolani Nkosi

These are the words of an 11-year old boy whose life was taken from him before he became a teenager. He died a year after delivering this message in a powerful speech at the 13th International Aids Conference held in Durban, South Africa, in July 2000. His address to the attendees was televised throughout the world.

His name at birth was Xolani Nkosi, but in the very short time that he lived, he would become known to millions as Nkosi Johnson—a young boy who was born in a township east of Johannesburg in 1989, HIV-positive—the virus passed on to him by his mother.

Nkosi's incredible journey is a courageous story of how he and his foster mother, Gail Johnson, turned rejection into direction and began to change not only his life but also the lives of others.

Serendipity would bring Gail and Nkosi together to begin their good work. Nkosi's birth mother, Daphne, became very ill. She and Nkosi entered into an AIDS care center in Johannesburg. Here is where fate brought Gail Johnson to Nkosi. She was a social worker at the center and became Nkosi's foster mom after Daphne died.

In 1997, Gail attempted to enroll then-eight-year-old Nkosi in a school in Melville, a suburb of Johannesburg. But opposition exploded when Nkosi's medical condition was revealed. Gail and Nkosi made no attempt to hide it; she'd actually brought attention to it through media interviews and public meetings. Parents who had children at the school were asked to vote on the issue—it resulted in a tie.

Finally the South African Parliament intervened. Voting almost unanimously, the government made it illegal for schools to prevent children who are HIV-positive from attending classes. The battle was won because Nokosi and Gail turned rejection into direction. They wouldn't accept "no." And because of their effort, Nkosi would get to go to school just like other kids.

The two were unstoppable—moving courageously and forcefully in a direction they hoped would create a better tomorrow for the millions of South Africans who were suffering from HIV/AIDS. They raised funds and fulfilled a dream: in April 1999 they opened Nkosi's Haven—a center that cares for HIV/AIDS mothers and their children so that they may remain together for as long as possible in an accepting and non-judgmental environment.

Nkosi passed away from an AIDS-related disease on June 1, 2001—but not before he had taken action, used rejection as cues for direction and done more good by the age of 11 than most of us will ever do in a lifetime.

Finding Direction in Rejection

What keeps some people from finding direction in rejection? The risk of failing. Successful people handle rejection differently from the way others do.

Successful people follow a recipe that they believe in their hearts will eventually bring them success. It's cultivated by a vision mentioned in the previous principle; I call it "Dreams, Purpose, and a Dedicated Plan" (DP-DP).

Internationally known speaker Brian Tracy refers to something similar that he calls "positive knowing," and uses the following analogy: When you get a new recipe you've never made before but maybe have tasted the dish at a restaurant, you *positively know* it can taste great. So now you go home and take all the ingredients and mix them up, and generally the first time it's not identical to what you tasted in the restaurant (in fact, sometimes it's barely edible). But you try again and again because you *positively know* those ingredients mixed together will create something delicious.

It's the same for successful people—they realize that following key principles every day will eventually bring their desired outcome.

DP-DP is the foundation for success. The Dream part of this acronym is about what you want in life. The Purpose is your reason for this desire—why must you accomplish it. The Dedicated Plan is your means to achieve it. Without DP-DP the chances are that you won't accomplish your desires (likely because you won't even know what your true passions are, nor even how to pursue them).

When we are young it's easy to believe in our dreams. Then as we get older we have doubts and think of reasons why we can't fulfill our dreams. Suddenly we lose our purpose, and before we even create a dedicated plan, we've talked ourselves out of sticking to it.

It's these emotions that make some people afraid to dream or put their vision on paper. Dreams, Purpose, and Dedicated Plans are replaced with fear and worry.

Many people believe that failing is the worst thing that can happen to us. But let's take a quick look at three people who persisted beyond failure, and made the world a better place because of their success: Jonas Salk, Charles Franklin Kettering, and Thomas Watson. If these three men had allowed their fear of failure to immobilize them, our lives would be much harder today.

Jonas Salk invented the polio vaccine. But it took him 200 tries. When asked how he felt about all those failures, he replied, "I have never failed anything in my life; I just learned 200 ways how NOT to vaccinate for polio."

It's an attitude and a choice. You choose how you respond to your failures. Perhaps you're familiar with the following phrase: "Failure is not an event, but rather a judgment of an event." You do not have to perceive failure as bad and therefore be fearful of it. You can let it be direction for you and no longer fear it. Successful people are not afraid of failing—

therefore attempting something *is possible.* Failure does not define us; rather how we respond to failure is what shapes our character.

Charles Kettering invented the electric automobile starter. It was first incorporated into the Cadillac in 1912, and resulted in phenomenal growth for the company. This device forever changed the auto industry. Kettering once said, "An inventor fails 999 times, and if he succeeds once, he's in. He treats his failures simply as practice shots."

Thomas Watson made my life as a journalist and millions of other peoples' lives far easier. He built IBM, International Business Machines Corporation, the world's largest manufacturer of electric typewriters and data-processing equipment. A powerful positive thinker, he's been quoted as saying: "If you want to succeed, double your failure rate."

These men, who made significant contributions to mankind, not only refused to fail, they also squashed rejection. They may have gotten used to hearing the word "no," but they never accepted it. Instead, rejection became direction for these successful people.

This next exercise is very helpful as you plan your future projects. I use it when I am contemplating small personal decisions as well as career choices. Answer the questions as specifically as possible on a separate piece of paper. Write what goal or outcome you want to achieve. Explain why this is important to you. For instance, you might write that you want to buy an investment property to help create supplemental revenue. The changes you may need to make can be as simple as taking investment real estate courses to help you make the best property choice. Sometimes the changes will also involve changing mental attitudes, such as believing that you can become a landlord and putting to rest the fear that it will be too much work. The action step in this exercise is similar to the one you completed on the topic of worry. Write down as many action steps as you can that will bring you closer to your desired outcome. Write down *everything.* You can determine later whether a certain action step is appropriate, but first just get it on paper. It's also important to know what the risk is if you don't achieve your desired outcome. This can act as an incentive to stop you from procrastinating. If you put off buying that investment property, what other stream of income can you rely on during your retirement?

Worriless Life Desired Outcome Exercise

Desired Outcome: What outcome do I want/intend to create?

Why: For what reason or purpose do I desire to achieve this outcome?

Changes: What changes in myself do I need to make?

Action: What actions will I take to achieve my outcome?

Risk: If I don't achieve the outcome, what are my risks?

Mantra

I turn rejection into direction. When I am told, "No," I find another way.

I have a purpose and am committed to my intentions to find the direction

that brings me successful living.

12. I Choose Peace

Do you ever feel like you are Dr. Jekyll and Mr. Hyde? Conflict stirs inside you, peace seems to elude you, and at times you turn into someone you don't even recognize—or want to even admit—is part of you? I think we've all been there. Maybe at work you're calm and easygoing. Then suddenly you come home from the office and the children are fighting or there's a big mess in the kitchen. Suddenly you feel the transformation taking place inside you—anger beginning to erupt. It's like Superman melting down because of exposure to kryptonite. The fact is that sometimes we are indeed a *very different person (conflicted, non-peaceful)*, when we are in certain environments. Choosing peace in those moments seems utterly impossible.

I have a good friend whose daughter's mother recently died. The nearly- teenage girl had not lived with her dad. Yet, literally overnight, my friend was becoming a full-time dad. His child was traveling thousands of miles away from her familiar surroundings and moving in with him. One day, not too long after the daughter moved in, this friend told me how he was struggling with parenting his daughter. There were screaming matches and lots of conflicts, most likely resulting from lifestyle changes for both people, and also the daughter's grief for the loss of her mother. His daughter needed "strong discipline," and "tough love," my friend told me. Frustrated, he contemplated his choices: routinely grounding his daughter, continuous yelling matches, etc. I suggested that more peaceful communication was needed—listening more in order to create less conflict in their household. I advocated love in all circumstances, and suggested that he provide guidance using a peaceful, caring, and respectful style, and strive to first understand her position before trying to get his point understood.

I knew my friend was a gentle person, good-natured, kind, and generally even-tempered. But the way he was talking about disciplining his daughter was the opposite. He felt he had to let his daughter know he was in control. My friend felt that, in order to raise his child correctly, he had to become someone other than who he really was. I explained to my friend that I had never seen him handle anyone in the manner he'd been describing. I then asked him why he felt he had to become a harsher person in order to raise a loving, respectful daughter. My friend only said it was what he thought his daughter needed.

Months later I received another call from this same friend. He had tried what I suggested and, instead of using an unauthentic, harsh style of dealing with his daughter, he dealt with her with the same respect that he used with his friends and co-workers—and what a difference it has made! Peace had replaced conflict. Now, when disagreements occurred, he chose peace first and calmly, through *actively* listening, found out the real issues that were troubling his daughter. Today their connection is stronger, their bond deeper because they respectfully communicate, *actively* listen to each other, and always choose peace first.

Actively rather than *passively* listening to someone during a conversation enables you to really understand what that person is trying to convey.

Oral communication is misunderstood more than half the time, which creates a greater likelihood for conflict. Much of that is because people do not *actively* listen; instead they have become accustomed to being *passive* listeners. The difference lies between *hearing* what someone says, and *listening* to what someone says. Listening requires effort—you are *actively* trying to hear. Hearing is merely perceiving sound through our ears. Sometimes people say, "I know you heard me, but you didn't listen to what I said." This would be considered *passive* listening.

Passive listening is what most of us do routinely without thinking. We hear things, but don't necessarily make an effort to absorb the meaning and relate it to any of our experiences. *Passive* listeners are often looking at the ceiling, the floor, out the window, at the computer screen, just about anywhere other than into the other person's eyes. Genuine communication doesn't happen in this situation; words just "go in one ear and out the other!"

Active listening is engaging. You are looking at the other person, attentively listening, and making an effort to understand the communication.

Active listening is a process of taking in the other person's words and converting them into meaningful information.

Whether we are dealing with our children, spouse, friends, or business associates, we often forget that respectful, peaceful communication, and *active* listening are not inherent; this is a skill that must be practiced. When we don't use it, we lose the ability to do it.

To Create Peaceful Communication, You Have to Listen

Have you ever had a conversation with someone, but felt like you were not really heard? It's as though that person was just waiting for you to finish talking so that he could begin. Chances are that you can count on one hand the number of people who have really listened carefully to you. Most of us aren't *active* listeners. We all have the ability to be *passive* listeners—physically present, but mentally absent. Being an *active* listener is critical to leading not only a peaceful life, but also a successful one.

As a reporter, I have listened to thousands of stories—seniors who get scammed, parents recounting tragic stories about the loss of their children, convicted killers proclaiming their innocence in court, fire victims sharing tales of mass destruction, politicians touting strategies to mend the world (and secure their re-election). After years of reporting, on a good day I was intrigued, *actively* listening to every word my interviewee had to say. On a bad day (maybe my daughter had been sick the night before and I was up most of the night or some other trouble was filling my head), I had to struggle to stay focused and not fall into a *passive* listening style—merely hearing the words, but not absorbing or retaining anything meaningful from them. Effort is required to *choose peace* in your life, just as effort is required to *actively* listen to people, especially when you are preoccupied. *Actively* listening is a rarely-practiced skill, but it's crucial for successful, peaceful living.

Responsible listening is the speaking we do to prove to the other person

that we understand what his or her total message said.

It saves us from attacking and defending.

It allows for no judgment of the other person's character.

It's only function is the present—what the speaker meant at this

moment—in this conversation. Listening is the suspension of

judgments— until we gain new information.

~Peter deLisser

10 Tips for Becoming an *Active* Listener

1. Aim to understand fully what the other person is saying

2. Suspend judgment; objectivity is critical to effective listening

3. Don't interrupt

4. Avoid formulating your next question, comment, or response in your head while the other person is talking

5. Engage your mind in the conversation

6. Look the other person in the eyes

7. If you are busy and cannot give your full attention, ask the person to speak to you later when you can give respectful, undivided attention

8. Lean forward, nod your head, involve your whole body in the process of *actively* listening

9. Take notes, if appropriate

10. After the person finishes speaking, reiterate what was said and ask for clarification if needed

If you're trying to listen and talk at the same time,

you'll stink at both of them.

~Kyle Nixon (at age 11)

Sometimes our own messages are delivered right back to us through someone not only close to us but even decades younger. We have to remember to listen not just to those in higher positions (or with whom we're trying to gain good favor) but also to those who may be perceived as knowing less or even unable to help us.

I went to the county fair with my daughter when she was eight. It was crowded and smelled of saturated deep-fried fatty foods that melt in your mouth but later take up permanent residence on your hips. The music was blaring, lights were flashing, carnival barkers were yelling, "Today only! Three balls—five dollars! Knock down any Coke can and win a prize. Did you *hear* what I said?" I heard and tried not to *actively* listen to the noisy hawking.

We headed for the rides and boarded the "Crazy Mouse." I can handle some roller coasters if they're fairly tame (I figured this one was). The ride began with some little hills and a not-too-alarming pace (I thought I was in the clear). And then suddenly, you'd have thought I was in Disneyland's twisting teacup ride! Around and around it went—slowly then fast, fast, faster. I crawled off the ride feeling sick and dragged myself to the bathroom.

Sitting on a toilet in the stall, I could feel my stomach still spinning and my head throbbing. My daughter's eyes filled with tears. "I'm scared, Mommy. How will you drive us home?"

I didn't quite know, but I struggled to whisper, "Don't worry, I'll be OK. I'll get us home." It must not have sounded too convincing because Siena tried another technique. Gathering her courage and forgetting her worries, she began creating a peaceful visual.

"Focus, Mommy, just focus on something positive, beautiful." Siena continued, "All you have to do is think about something pretty and fun like a farm and you're sitting on a haystack watching the cows graze. The ducks are swimming in the pond and you can feel the cool air."

I listened as *actively* as possible in that condition. I was beginning to get the picture in my head. (Funny thing, I never knew that my city girl knew so much about farms.)

She went on, "Inside the house mommies are making cakes. The children are playing outside. The mommy horse is feeding its babies. Think about how beautiful it is there."

I got the picture. Siena had used visualization as her tool, and peaceful communication as her means to help me forget about the nausea.

It worked. I drove us home, still a little sick, but happier because Siena could see how her efforts kept me focused and on track, and how respectful, peaceful communication can bring positive changes. At home she put me to bed and then lay down next to me, face-to-face. I thanked her for what she had done. She said, "When I care about people I try to do what's right for them." I thought to myself, What an amazing girl I have! And then she said, "Do you think maybe, Mommy, that you should sleep facing the other way? You know, just in case you get sick?" And I thought, A smart girl, too!

Being listened to is so close to being loved

that most people cannot tell the difference.

~David Oxberg

Mantra

I know that in all circumstances it is my option to choose peace—I choose to embrace peace and eliminate conflict. In all conversations I actively listen to gain meaningful information.

13.   I Leave the Buts Behind
(or they'll only get bigger!)

He that is good for making excuses is seldom good for anything else.

~ Benjamin Franklin

A lot of us continually make excuses as to why we can't have the life we want. To live successfully we need to *leave the buts behind, or they will only get bigger.* Every excuse you make prepares you for yet another one and serves only to delay your success. They are roadblocks in the path to success.

Excuses allow you to forget or pretend that you are not responsible for your success or failure. The important first step in this principle is to begin to accept that your life is the way it is *because of you.* You are responsible for your happiness and success. And you are responsible if you hate your life and are unsuccessful. Excuses only serve to allow you to duck responsibility.

When you recognize that your life is in your own hands and you can determine whether you succeed or fail, you give yourself power to choose and competence to take action. You have more self-respect when you take full responsibility for things that happen to you in your life.

Some people act as though their life is like that toy, the Rubik's Cube. The cube starts off perfectly aligned and balanced when you take it out of its package, but, like our lives, we can mess it up quickly. In no time at all you turn it left, then right, up, and then down—and before you know it, the cube is a mismatch of colors—and you have no idea how it got that way or how to get it back into alignment. Life can be like that. We move in various directions, often not evaluating our actions and choices. Good decisions make us happy; for bad decisions we make excuses, rationalize, and blame others. This behavior is a dead end for success.

Leave the buts behind by ridding your life of counterproductive behavior such as criticism and blame. Instead be responsible, action-oriented, and ambitious.

Make a decision to always be the kind of person you can trust. Don't play the victim or dwell in pity. Know that you can change your life because you are responsible for the way it is today.

I loved how actress Teri Hatcher—a star in *Desperate Housewives*—turned her life around. The once-has-been actress thought her career was over after a multiple-year slump.

Hatcher said in an interview that she "was really used to being a survivor of bad things." But when she turned 40, Hatcher tried on a new attitude—and opportunity came knocking. She took the role of Susan Mayer, a struggling single mother. It re-launched her career in the limelight. No more excuses or accepting that her career was over.

At an awards ceremony she humbly told the audience, "Thank you so much for giving me a chance when I couldn't have been a bigger has-been."

Hatcher proved she could "Leave the buts behind before they get bigger." And it's something you can do, too.

What "but" do you need to leave behind?

I really want to drop 20 pounds "but" it's just genetic for me to be heavy. I wanted to go to the event "but" I just got too busy. I really wish I were out of debt "but" I just can't save money. These excuses will undermine a person's character and self-esteem. The more you make excuses, the larger the excuses get. At first it might be an excuse for being late such as I would have been on time to work "but" there was heavy traffic. With more practice using "but" it soon turns into I hate my job and would have changed careers, "but" I'm just too old, not qualified, not certified, etc. Don't underestimate the power of "but"—it can halt success instantly. Accepting responsibility for what you do—good or bad decisions—will make you a stronger, more respectable person. When you "leave the buts behind," you find that you build greater trust with others because you are no longer making excuses, instead you're telling the truth.

And once you tell the truth, you can determine what is really blocking your success. For instance, if you want to change careers and are not doing it, what is really holding you back? It's likely to be worry and fear. Understand that you can apply reason and logic to your fears and allow them to dissipate.

If you don't have the certification you need for a new career, you can research the position and begin to get the information you need to decide if this is the route for you. But your career growth will be stunted if you continue to make excuses instead of taking action.

Start today by choosing to *leave the buts behind*. Accept the consequences that go along with giving up excuses; learn from your mistakes. Hold yourself accountable to a higher standard, and your life will be greatly enriched. Giving up the "buts" makes room for treasures in your life—and reveals the authentic you.

Worriless Life Exercise

Write down your biggest "but" _____

_____

_____

_____

_____

How has this "but" affected your life? _____

_____

_____

_____

_____

What's the truth behind the "but"? _____

_____   _____

_____

_____

If this "but" were no longer used as an excuse, how would your life be better?

_____

_____

_____

_____

Are you willing to give up this "but"?   YES / NO

If not now, WHEN?

Mantra

I Take Out the Trash and with it all of my excuses.

I realize that every time I rid myself of my excuses,

I bring successful living and harmony into my life.

I am responsible for my life.

14. I Laugh Out Loud Daily

Go Ahead Laugh a Little—or Better Yet, a Lot

Often we discover that something is missing in our lives. It's a curious phenomenon that occurs: the transition from child to adult often depletes our sense of humor and replaces it with worry. We take life and ourselves too seriously.

During a vacation I learned that one of the most important characteristics to keep intact is my sense of humor. In fact, studies show that laughter boosts the immune system, reduces fatigue by 87 percent, and generally helps people better deal with stressful situations.

One Christmas I vacationed in Twain Harte, California (a town in the Sierra Nevada Mountains), with my daughter and her girlfriend. We'd been there two days and had not yet skied. So despite the heavy storm that was blowing in, we headed out to the nearby ski resort. Little did we know that we were destined for *A Series of Unfortunate Events.*

The snow was coming down fast, blanketing the pine trees. After getting two kids fed, taking care of bathroom runs, loading up the car, more bathroom runs, and satisfying the last-minute cries of "I'm hungry," we finally got a very late start up the hill to Dodge Ridge.

A battle with the snow chains—one apparently had gotten bent and was destined to come loose every few feet—slowed our journey, but it didn't really dampen our spirits. We were going skiing!

Only five miles from the lodge, we were in a steady stream of traffic, until the car in front of us decided to quickly brake on the snow-covered road. We had to swerve slightly to avoid hitting the car. In a matter of moments the front end of our car was securely settled into a snowy embankment—we were stuck.

It's amazing how many things can go wrong when you're on your way to doing something fun. But even more amazing is how much fun you *can* have in spite of your circumstances.

Watch kids and notice that they laugh—a lot. In fact, some statistics show they actually laugh 400 times a day, compared to adults who choose to stifle their own giggles and end up laughing an average of only 15 times a day.

So it's not surprising that in difficult situations, a lot can be learned from children. While we were stuck, the girls were giggling, playing in the snow, building an igloo (in case we had to stay for the night, they told us). The girls did not worry in the slightest that our day on the slopes was gradually slipping away. No, they were having fun in the midst of life's zingers; just taking life for what it offered and relishing the present moment.

Seeing the girls' delight in life's simple and free pleasures made me think about how our fast-paced society is becoming driven by the need for more, newer, and increasingly extravagant *toys*. And adults can actually be worse than kids when it comes to supporting the production of top-line gadgets, fully loaded cars, and trinkets that claim to simplify our lives. (Of course you have to read the 85-page, fine-print manual first.)

So resolve, right now, to lighten your heart—it could just be the missing link to living well.

(By the way, we made it to the slopes that day in time to eat and find out that the ski lifts closed in 40 minutes. So we took our cue from the kids and pulled out the sleds, and played for free. Thank goodness I have a 10-year-old to remind me how to *live well!*)

Love is Spelled T-I-M-E

I went with my girlfriend, Sophie, to get her one-year-old son Dominic's hair cut. Memories instantly flooded my mind. It was about nine years ago that my daughter was sitting in one of those stationary cars with a very animated and friendly hairdresser standing over her and attempting to do the impossible—snip a little here and a little there—all the while, I videotaped every second (as an obsessed new mom does with her first child!).

Time passes very quickly; kids graduate from diapers to college in a flash. That's why, as I reflect on years gone by, I feel particularly good about how much time I spent with my daughter. I know that she'll soon be looking for ways to "hang out" only with her friends, and I'll have to book an appointment with her.

Schedules are busy and life is typically never as simple as we would like it to be. But once time is gone, you can't get it back. This year I've made a pledge to spend more time with those I love. After all, love is spelled T-I-M-E. It's something you can't buy or replace—you just have to give it freely and when you don't have enough of it, you have to find a way to prioritize things in your life so that you do have enough time for those who are really important to you.

"You've got to schedule time with your family," Adam Christing from Clean Comedians told me. Christing makes people laugh for a living, but he finds it no laughing matter that some kids are missing out on family time.

"Don't be a spectator; get involved. You might feel kind of dorky bowling with your kids, but they'll love it. If the kid bowls a strike and you bowl a gutter ball, that might be the highlight of the year," Christing explained.

He encourages parents to develop hobbies together and, perhaps most of all, to laugh together.

"Someone said that the shortest distance between two people is a smile, so I think that when you laugh with your family, it relieves a lot of stress and tension and just creates some great memories," Christing said.

Laughter does more than that. As previously mentioned, medical researchers have found that laughter actually boosts the immune system. It's quite obvious that children laugh far more than adults; just visit any school playground for confirmation. But it's not that we grow old and stop laughing; rather, we stop laughing and grow old.

There is a cure. It's called "L-P-M" or Laughs Per Minute, a theory that Christing uses in his comedy performances. He makes it a goal to deliver five Laughs Per Minute, and at that rate, he's sure to leave his audience healthier than when they walked through the door.

Laugh out loud. Make it a habit not to take yourself or the circumstances in your life so seriously. Remember Principle #8: *I Know This Too Shall Pass.*

Mantra

I laugh and live freely. I accept that there will be challenges. I face them bravely with humor and gratitude for what I already have accomplished. I realize that every chuckle helps me to create the life I intend to live.

Daily Mantras and Corresponding Principles

1. I Choose to Be Successful

2. I Ask, "Why Not?"

3. I Know What I am Fighting For

4. I Take Action!

5. I Practice Forgiveness and Tolerance

6. I Acknowledge My Emotions

7. I Create Positive Expectations

8. I Know This Too Shall Pass

9. I Answer the Door When Opportunity Knocks

10. I Take My Eyes off the Rearview Mirror

11. I Turn Rejection into Direction

12. I Choose Peace

13. I Leave the Buts Behind (or they'll only get bigger!)

14. I Laugh Out Loud Daily

1. *I choose an optimistic attitude. What I focus on I will attain. I choose to be successful, transforming woes to wonders. I choose to be a catalyst, creating success in my life and the lives of those I meet—and even those I may never know.*

2. *I ask, "Why not?" I am open to receiving new ideas, information, and opportunity—through an inquisitive mind, a soul filled with hope and faith, I welcome the chance to learn and try things that I have never done before. I invite creative collaboration into my life.*

3. *I have a mission in life. I live successfully. I know what I am fighting for, and am committed to succeeding. I understand that at times I may feel disconnected from my purpose, but I have the power to reconnect and awaken the spirit in me that knows what I am fighting for.*

4. *I take action, no matter how small or big. I recognize that everything I do matters to my life, to those I know, and to those I may never know. I am responsible for my choices and behavior. I make decisions and take action in a timely fashion.*

5. *I open my heart to forgiveness and know that justice comes only from within. I hold only the precious memories that serve me well. I practice patience, tolerance, and understanding—I am completely successful and richly rewarded when my heart is open to receive.*

6. *I acknowledge my feelings as part of life's experiences. I choose my reactions. I am mindful of my feelings and know that they can easily be ignited. But, through careful consideration, I select the behavior and thoughts that guarantee me successful living.*

7. *I create positive expectations. What I desire I will acquire. What I believe, I will live; therefore, I fill my mind with thoughts that support my intentions of successful living. I surround myself with optimistic people.*

8. *I know that I will survive. In fearful or sad moments I remember that this too shall pass. I remember my moments of joy and can reconnect to them. I focus on solutions that bring greater success into my life.*

9. *I have many opportunities and my options are plentiful. I invite good things and good people into my life, and then gladly open the door to receive them.*

10. *I recognize that my past is behind me and that now, in the present, I create my destiny. I clear away old, negative mental clutter and accept new, positive messages in its place.*

11. *I turn rejection into direction. When I am told, "No," I find another way. I have a purpose and am committed to my intentions to find the direction that brings me successful living.*

12. *I know that in all circumstances it is my option to choose peace—I choose to embrace peace and eliminate conflict. In all conversations I actively listen to gain meaningful information.*

13. *I Take Out the Trash and with it all of my excuses. I realize that every time I rid myself of my excuses, I bring successful living and harmony into my life. I am responsible for my life.*

14. *I laugh and live freely. I accept that there will be challenges. I face them bravely with humor and gratitude for what I already have accomplished. I realize that every chuckle helps me to create the life I intend to live.*

Let us all work to discover our deepest levels of respectful connection with each other. Let us create what we intend, and recognize that if we strive for peace, we will live in harmony.

I wish you successful living—what you do matters—you are impacting the world in which we all live. God Bless. Namaste.